Still Counting

Meditations for Senior Adults

Frances Simpson

Celebrate the years!

Frances Simpson

Still Counting – Meditations for Senior Adults

CrossLink Publishing
www.crosslink.org

Copyright © 2009 by Frances Simpson

All rights reserved. No part of this book may be reproduced or transmitted in any form or by any means without written permission of the author.

Printed in the United States of America. All rights reserved under International Copyright Law.

ISBN 978-0-9816983-7-3

All scripture quotations, unless otherwise indicated, are taken from the *Holy Bible, New International Version*®. NIV®. Copyright © 1973, 1978, 1984 by International Bible Society. Used by permission of Zondervan. All rights reserved.

Scripture quotations from *THE MESSAGE*. Copyright © by Eugene H. Peterson 1993, 1994, 1995, 1996, 2000, 2001, 2002. Used by permission of NavPress Publishing Group.

Scripture quotations marked "NKJV" are taken from the New King James Version. Copyright © 1982 by Thomas Nelson, Inc. Used by permission. All rights reserved.

This book is dedicated to

senior adults everywhere

who are learning to count their blessings

in the classroom of life

Acknowledgements

I thank my husband, Eugene Simpson, who provided the material for many of these meditations and who faithfully counts the years with me.

I salute our children and grandchildren who have filled the years with love, laughter, and a few anxious moments: our son Mark, his wife Lori, and their children, Erin and Emily; our daughter Karen, her husband Al, and their children, David, Brittany, and Jacob. You will find them in many of my stories.

I appreciate all the senior adults who have influenced my life for as long as I can remember. You will meet some of them in these pages.

I pray for all of you who read these meditations, that you will keep adding, subtracting, multiplying, and dividing as Jesus, the Master Teacher, adds up the dividends.

Thanks to my friend Ernestine Blackwell, who read the manuscript and gave constructive comments; to Anne Panaccione, who tutored me in computer techniques; and to Steve Hardman, who keeps my computer running.

Still Counting

Teach us to number our days aright,
that we may gain a heart of wisdom.
Psalm 90:12

ADDING

SUBTRACTING

MULTIPLYING

DIVIDING

75 AND STILL COUNTING

At age 75, most of my life is history, and the pages of my earthly calendar are filling up fast. I have few complaints, and my doctor tells me I'm healthy for my age. Nevertheless, against the backdrop of eternity, life is like a "mist that appears for a little while and then vanishes" (James 4:14b).

Where have the years gone? Some were so busy they flew by like a blur on life's screen. Some pages are orderly and neat. Others reveal an unsteady hand, an uncertain slant. Together, they tell the story of my life.

Looking back is not my objective these days, though nostalgia does creep in occasionally. My question is: How does God want me to live the remaining months and years of my life?

From this question have emerged these writings about matters that are important to senior adults. Throughout these pages you will see God at work adding virtues and meaning to life while subtracting those things that are not good for us. He multiplies what we give to Him and helps us divide the good from the bad so we can make right choices.

I pray that these meditations will help you as much as they have helped me.

Table of Contents

Adding

For this very reason, make every effort
to add to your faith goodness;
and to goodness, knowledge;
and to knowledge, self-control;
and to self-control, perseverance;
and to perseverance, godliness;
and to godliness, brotherly kindness;
and to brotherly kindness, love.
For if you possess these qualities
in increasing measure,
they will keep you from
being ineffective and unproductive
in your knowledge of our Lord Jesus Christ.

2 Peter 1:5-8

Frances Simpson

IT'S STILL GOOD

In the beginning of time, God looked upon the world He had made and "saw that it was good" (Gen. 1:10b). Today, I look at my backyard domain and say, "It's still good."

Okay, it's not manicured as well as my husband and I would like (age does make a difference). The grass is brown here and there (common for July in our area); but, for my husband and me, it's our Garden of Eden.

From our deck, we watch cardinals and monarch butterflies flit across the yard. Squirrels and rabbits come out to play each evening. Zinnias, hydrangea, and roses color the landscape. The pines, holly trees, and poplars form a bulwark against the nearby traffic. It's an ever-changing scene of quiet beauty and mystery – buds open, acorns fall, and leaves turn. Some days, rain pelts our outdoor paradise. Occasionally, snow feathers it. But always, the sunshine returns and the breezes find our corner.

The four seasons, in our part of the world, reveal God's glory in varied colors and designs. One season ushers in another as the growing cycle takes place, the land rests, then is renewed to start all over again. Every season has its time and place. What is your favorite – spring, summer, autumn, or winter?

There are cycles in other areas of life, too. Seasons of the soul have their brown deserts and stormy days mingled with Easter mornings and productive summers. Seasons of life are interwoven, each one enhancing the other. Looking back, it's all been good.

With the Psalmist I cry out, "The heavens declare the glory of God; the skies proclaim the work of his hands" (Psalm 19:1).

Creator God, thank You for speaking to me through my backyard world today. It tells me You are a God of beauty, order, and design. Thank you for creating me to enjoy it.

A TRIBUTE TO MARRIAGE

This year my husband and I will celebrate our 55th wedding anniversary. A lot has happened in this more than half a century. From the church-packed wedding, to our surprise 25th anniversary party, to our 50th year celebration, we have now arrived older, slower, and, hopefully, a little wiser.

Looking back, it has been an eventful journey, a fast journey. I would label it all "good," but then I remember a few detours and some bumps along the way. Tough decisions, financial need, misunderstandings, cancer, and many other things have crossed our paths. Still, I want to shout to the world, "It's a good life."

Jesus said, "I have come that they may have life, and have it to the full" (John 10:10b). In the depths of my being, I exclaim, "Amen."

Some people experience difficult, unhappy marriages, and the memories are not always good. God wants to make them better. His path to recovery is paved with forgiveness, mercy, and love.

Unlike many women my age, I still have the joy of sharing life with my husband. Our times together these days are quieter, more thoughtful, laced with contentment. We reminisce about family and friends, the churches we've pastored, the places we've been. My husband and I are both planners; so not long ago, we made a list of 50 things we want to do before we die. We are working on them.

Though we both enjoy personal pursuits, we are one entity, joined by God, to care for each other until "death do us part."

O God, thank You for my husband and the years we've grown together. As the future presents new challenges and raises more questions, keep us "one in the bond of love."

Frances Simpson

AN ODE TO CHILDREN

Children grow up so fast – from diapers to tricycles to automobiles – from kindergarten to high school to college. Before you know it, they move out and have children of their own. During the process, time seems to hang on; however, from today's vantage point, things went too fast. None of us can unravel the past, but we can learn from it and do better.

The older I get the more I realize that having adult children nearby is an added bonus. As parents, our job is not to interfere, give unsolicited advice, or crowd the schedule, but to enjoy. Listen and encourage as you share birthday celebrations, shopping trips, and church functions with your children. When you need them, they will be there for you.

For those of us who have children in faraway places, keeping family close becomes a challenge, one that we have more time for than they do. I write letters, send cards, e-mail, and talk on the phone. Still, I cherish the times when I can look into the eyes of those I love, see them smile, and reach out to touch. Recently our son, in a distant city, flew to Florida to meet us for the 50th anniversary of a church we had pastored! What joy!

As Christians, we have been adopted into God's family, and He wants to spend quality time with us. "Practice the Presence of Jesus" is more than a cliché. It becomes an exciting adventure as we walk in fellowship with Him.

The Psalmist wrote, "Sons are a heritage from the Lord, children a reward from him" (Psalm 127:3). I like God's family plan. It's a good one.

O God, thank you for my children, my son and daughter, who are as much a part of me today as when I first cradled them in my arms. Thank you for the love that binds across the miles and for the hugs that reach across town.

GRANDPARENTING IS FUN

I knew I was a grandmother the day Erin Paige was born. But months later, when she crossed the threshold of our home, I accumulated some evidence – small handprints on the patio door, a crayoned picture, a sticky desktop. Some new images were etched on my mind – a bundle of energy wrapped in yellow pajamas, small arms enfolding a black and white dog, a sleeping beauty curved inside a borrowed baby bed. Grandchildren elicit a special kind of love and give us occasions to spoil with no strings attached.

Some grandparents do not have a hands-on relationship with their grandchildren while others are pulled into the care circle more than they want to be. Whatever our situation, God knows and cares about our offspring more than we do. The Psalmist wrote, "But from everlasting to everlasting the Lord's love is with those who fear him, and his righteousness with their children's children" (Psalm 103:17).

How do you stay close to your grandchildren? One thing I enjoy doing is compiling a photograph/scrapbook for each grandchild. On birthdays, I write a letter to be added to the book. It was fun to watch Brittany, our fifteen-year-old, as we celebrated her birthday recently. After she blew out her candles and opened her gifts, I read her birthday letter to her. Then, she took down her special book, lay on the floor, and pulled her mother (our daughter) alongside to review the story of her life. It was fun to hear the giggles, the ooh's and ah's.

The most important role we have, as grandparents, is to make sure our grandchildren's spiritual birthdays are recorded in the Lamb's Book of Life. What an awesome responsibility we have!

Dear Father, thank You for the privilege of being called "Grandma."

Frances Simpson

I LOVE THE CHURCH

When I was ten years old, a church in a nearby town came to the village where I lived, pitched a tent one-half block from our house, and held a protracted meeting. Out of curiosity, I attended the services and felt engulfed in the warmth and enthusiasm of the people.

When the meeting was over, the group erected a building and called a pastor. Since my parents did not attend church at that time, I kept going. During the first revival in the new sanctuary, I knelt at the altar and gave my heart to Christ. The following Sunday I joined the church.

After graduation from high school, I attended a church college, where I met and married a ministerial student. For 55 years now we have lived and breathed "church."

"Christ loved the church and gave himself up for her" (Eph. 5:25b). I love the church, too. The church is my spiritual family, my feeding place, and my deployment center.

For some older folks, church is not like it used to be. Those with hearing problems, like my husband, cannot enjoy the music, hear the testimonies, or feel the flow of the service. Some cannot stand for long. I, for one, cannot kneel at the altar. Many of us cannot drive at night, which limits our church attendance. Nevertheless, we need the church and the church needs us.

Look around your church next Sunday and see if there is something you can do to help. If so, volunteer. Greet newcomers and take them out to lunch. Boost your pastor, your music leader, and your Sunday School teacher. We are the church; let's make it better.

Dear Heavenly Father, thank You for making me a spiritual being so that I can know and worship You. You are my dwelling place.

THE ADVENTURE OF PRAYER

Jesus made some bold statements about prayer. On one occasion, He said to a group gathered around Him on a mountainside, "Ask and it will be given to you; seek and you will find; knock and the door will be opened to you" (Matt. 7:7). James wrote, "The prayer of a righteous man is powerful and effective" (James 5:16b). Taken singularly, promises like this might lead us to pray selfishly or presumptuously.

R.A. Torrey's book, *The Power of Prayer*, has helped me to understand prayer better. I can't get away from his statement, "Prayer is the key that unlocks all the storehouses of God's infinite grace and power. All that God is, and all that God has, is at the disposal of prayer."[i] This makes me want to shout.

Mr. Torrey then goes on to lay out some guidelines for effective praying. He emphasizes the need for definite and determined prayer. We must study God's Word to find His will in any given situation. Then, we can pray, in faith, believing that He will answer. This sounds like hard work, and it is. It's not that we wrestle with God but we do confront the devil and his forces.

When I was 16, my father had a major heart attack. As he lay near death, I slipped out the back door of our house, knelt in the snow by a wash bench, and asked God to give my dad one more chance to get ready for heaven. For 15 years, God worked on answering that prayer. The last two years of Dad's life I fasted every Monday as I prayed for him. I wrote letters and sent scriptures outlining the plan of salvation. Dad was saved ten months before he died at the age of 52. What an adventure in prayer!

Dear Jesus, thank You for teaching us how to pray. Thank You for the answers You have orchestrated just for me. I approach Your throne today with anticipation and praise.

THE BIBLE SPEAKS

God speaks to us in many ways. He speaks through nature, through the prompting of the Holy Spirit, through open and closed doors, through other people. In Old Testament times, He spoke through angels and visions. The most important way in which God speaks to us today is through the Bible. If any other voice differs from that of the Bible, it is not an authentic Word from God.

What does the Bible mean to you at this stage of your life? Do you have to read a large print edition or listen to audiotapes? As you read, is there an example to follow? An error to avoid? A command to obey? A promise to claim? A prayer to echo?

I like the way evangelist Billy Sunday outlined the Bible. He referred to the portico of Genesis, the Old Testament art gallery, the music room of Psalms, the business house of Proverbs, the observatory of the prophets. In the New Testament we enter the audience room of the King of Kings, take a trip through the Acts of the Apostles, linger a while in the Correspondence room, and then ascend into the throne room of Revelation.

To get the most out of reading our Bible, the American Bible Society suggests:

1. Read expectantly and thoughtfully.
2. Read with imagination, unhurried.
3. Conserve the results of your reading by keeping a notebook or journal.

The Psalmist declares, “I have hidden your word in my heart that I might not sin against you” (Psalm 119:11). The Bible is our textbook, our teaching manual, our roadmap to heaven. Handle it carefully.

O God, thank You for speaking to me through Your Word today. Thank you for the inspiration and guidance that it brings to my life.

COME, HOLY SPIRIT

Jesus talked with His disciples about many things as He traveled with them throughout Galilee – teaching in their synagogues, casting out demons, and healing the sick. On more than one occasion, He told them He was going away, back to the Father. There He would prepare a place for them so they could all be together again.

On the night before His crucifixion, Jesus expounded on the subject by announcing, "I will ask the Father, and he will give you another Counselor to be with you forever – the Spirit of truth" (John 14:16-17). "I will not leave you as orphans," He said (v. 18).

The second chapter of Acts records the coming of the Holy Spirit on the Day of Pentecost when the Christian Church was born and thrust into the world. Today, the Holy Spirit continues His work of conviction, regeneration, and empowerment for holy living. The Holy Spirit is "Christ in us," as Comforter, Counselor, Teacher, and Helper.

Dr. Fletcher Spruce wrote in one of his *Standard* articles, "The power of Pentecost is not the power to do a miracle – it is the power to be a miracle."

I've read the story of Henrietta Mears, Founder of Gospel Light Publications, who tells how she searched the Bible and closeted herself in prayer until, by faith, she reached out to receive the transforming power of the Holy Spirit. She described the experience as a flood of light that illuminated every corner of her life and became the controlling insight of all that she did.

Jesus said, "If you . . . . know how to give good gifts to your children, how much more will your Father in heaven give the Holy Spirit to those who ask him!" (Luke 11:13).

What do you need from the Holy Spirit today? Reach out and receive Him.

Come, Holy Spirit, I need You.

Frances Simpson

SUNDAY ETIQUETTE

"Remember the Sabbath Day by keeping it holy," (Exodus 20:8) God thundered from Mt. Sinai as He began to build a people through whom He could reveal himself to the world. So, how do we, as senior adults, approach Sunday, the Christian Sabbath?

First and foremost, Sunday is to be a day of worship and rest. It's a day for church, for family and friends, for enjoying nature and meditating on God's goodness. Jesus said, "it is lawful to do good on the Sabbath" (Matt. 12:12b). That opens up all kinds of possibilities for senior adults.

Jesus also said, "The Sabbath was made for man, not man for the Sabbath" (Mark 2:27a). In other words, we need the Sabbath. A group of researchers at Harvard Medical School did an experiment to determine the time required for nerves to react to certain stimuli. The team discovered that Sunday, as a day of rest or change, made a significant difference. On Monday the nerve reactions were high; by Saturday they were at their lowest point. The following Monday they were back to top performance.

For older adults who are homebound or in care facilities, I'm glad that worship can take place anywhere – in a wheel chair by the window, while lying in a hospital bed, or caring for a sick spouse. Many churches tape their worship services and take them to shut-ins during the week. Perhaps this is a ministry you can be involved in.

Worship and rest – that sounds good to me, at my age. Worship brings us into the vestibule of heaven and allows us to look into the holy of holies. It fills us with praise and reaches out to those around us. Our bodies may be racked with pain. Our memory may be fading. But we can worship God anytime of the day or night.

Dear Father, thank You for Sundays, my favorite day of the week.

FAITH IN ACTION

Webster's Dictionary defines faith as a firm belief or trust in any person, thing, or statement. It need not be a religious virtue. Faith says to the farmer, "Sow your seed"; to the pilot, it says, "Trust your instruments"; to the sailor, it says, "Hoist your sail."

Those who scoff at religious faith say, "I can't see or touch God, so I don't believe."

Neither do we see air in a balloon, nor the pull of gravity; we don't see love, or IQ's, or the breath of a baby.

"Oh, but we see the evidence," says the critic. If you are looking for proof of a Creator God, take a look at the world around you; measure the universe; study the human heart.

Hebrews says, "without faith it is impossible to please God, because anyone who comes to him must believe that he exists and that he rewards those who earnestly seek him" (Hebrews 11:6).

For the Christian, faith is complete confidence in Who God is. It's taking the Bible at face value. Glaphre Gilliland in her book, *When the Pieces Don't Fit*, pictures God as saying, "You believe more in what you aren't than in what I AM." [ii]

In a way, faith is like a boomerang. As we use what we have, it comes back to us in greater measure. Faith liberates, empowers, encourages, and heals. Faith makes the puzzles of life fit together and erases a lot of unnecessary questions.

Do you like to sing songs about faith? Join in – "Living by faith in Jesus above; Trusting, confiding in His great love; Safe from all harm in His sheltering arm, I'm living by faith and feel no alarm" (*Living by Faith* by James Wells).

O God, may the faith, on which I've stood for so many years, hold me steady in these days of my life.

LOVE IS THE GREATEST

How would you define love? Is it the warm feelings you share with the special folks in your life? Is it the bond that cements your best relationships? Is it the quiet contentment that comes when you are with certain people?

In her autobiography, *The Story of My Life*, Helen Keller tells how, as a deaf and blind child, she finally grasped the meaning of love from her teacher, Anne Sullivan. She described it as an invisible line stretched between her spirit and the spirits of others.

This invisible love can be experienced in so many ways – a child's embrace, tears in the eyes of a listening friend, a touch in the dark, a whispered, "I'll be praying for you."

The Bible tells us, "God is love. Whoever lives in love lives in God, and God in him" (1 John 4:16b). God's love is not a sentimental emotion. It's not something we can earn or seek. It penetrates Genesis through Revelation and reaches to where you and I live. Creation pictures God's love; the Cross spells it out; Heaven will seal it.

All ages thrive on love. Children reach out to receive it. Teenagers look for it. Senior adults need it. Love is God's image in us. Let's multiply it by giving it away – a card to a shut-in, a smile to the downcast lady in the hospital waiting room, a cherry pie for a harried mother. Love is an emotion that needs a face. It needs hands and feet that say, "I really do care."

First Corinthians 13 describes Christian love. Many of us can quote it, but living it out is a different matter. It's not easy to be patient, kind, and humble in all of life's circumstances. Maybe we should read the chapter again and make a checklist of things to pray about.

O God, help me to pass on your gift of love to someone today.

AMAZING GRACE

Grace is a multi-faceted word. *Webster's Encyclopedia of Dictionaries* lists several definitions and connotations – charm, refined motion, a short prayer of thanksgiving before a meal, a period of delay granted as a favor, an embellished musical note, the title used when addressing a duke or archbishop. The reason grace is such a beautiful word to me is that it also means "divine favor." I bask in God's grace daily and see it evidenced in the lives of those around me.

God's grace brought the Israelites through the Red Sea, rescued Daniel from the hungry lions, and saved Shadrach, Meshach, and Obednego from the fiery furnace. Grace is God spelled out in Jesus – His sinless life, His teachings, His Atonement for the sins of the world. Because of divine grace, Christ healed lepers, fed a crowd with five loaves and two fish, raised Lazarus from death. Divine grace welcomed me to a small church in southern Alabama, where I, too, met Christ.

As the learned and wealthy John Seldon lay dying, he turned to Archbishop Usher and said, "I have surveyed most of the learning that is among the sons of men, and my study is filled with books and manuscripts on various subjects. But at present I cannot recollect any passage out of all my books and papers whereon I can rest my soul, save this one from the sacred Scriptures:

"'For the grace of God that brings salvation has appeared to all men'" (Titus 2:11).[iii]

John Newton, the former slave trader, expressed it triumphantly, "Amazing grace! how sweet the sound That saved a wretch like me! I once was lost, but now am found; was blind, but now I see" (*Amazing Grace* by John Newton).

Dear God, thank You for your grace that covers me today.

THE CLOAK OF KINDNESS

I don't see a lot of articles on kindness. I know that kindness is part of being good, merciful, and forgiving; however, kindness itself is a virtue. "Be kind and compassionate to one another," Peter writes to Christians (Eph. 4:32a).

I love the story about an elderly woman and her grandson, Tommy, who spent the day at the zoo. As they waited in line for Tommy to get his cheeks painted by a local artist, a girl behind them pointed at Tommy and said, "You have too many freckles; there's no place to paint." Embarrassed, Tommy dropped his head.

"I love your freckles," Grandmother exclaimed, as she knelt down beside her grandson. Gently she traced her fingers across his cheeks. "Freckles are beautiful," she said as she stood up.

"Really?" the little boy asked.

"Of course," Grandmother replied, "Why, what could be prettier than freckles?"

Tommy thought for a moment, then stared into his grandma's face. Softly he whispered, "Wrinkles." Kindness works for all ages.

Kindness can ease the pain of a hurting friend. It can build a bridge to lonely people. It can mellow a family disagreement and pave the way for reconciliation. It works in churches, neighborhoods, and business meetings, too.

What's your kindness quotient? As we get older, pain, boredom, and dementia can cloud our thinking and affect the things we do and say. I believe God understands at such times. Hopefully, those around us do too.

O Lord, clothe me with kindness so that I can bring warmth and healing to someone who needs me today.

SPREAD SOME JOY

What words do you use to describe your highest moments – joy, happiness, pleasure?

Though the dictionary overlaps the meaning of the words, they do have different connotations. Pleasure is usually a temporary emotion caused by outside stimuli. Happiness, too, depends, in part, on life's circumstances. Joy, on the other hand, is deeper and more lasting – flowing, not so much from what is going on around us, but from well springs of the heart.

I enjoy studying different themes throughout the Bible. One that I have researched is *joy*. Using more than 40 scriptures, I came to some simple conclusions.

1. Real joy comes from the Lord – "for the joy of the Lord is your strength" (Nehemiah 8:10b).
2. Joy connects with other people – "I have no greater joy than to hear that my children are walking in the truth" (3 John:4).
3. Joy looks to the future – "and the ransomed of the Lord will return. They will enter Zion with singing; everlasting joy will crown their heads. Gladness and joy will overtake them, and sorrow and sighing will flee away" (Isaiah 35:10).

St. Cyprian, a third-century martyr, wrote to his friend Donatus, "It is a bad world, Donatus, an incredibly bad world. But I have discovered in the midst of it a quiet and holy people who have learned a great secret. They have found a joy which is a thousand times better than any pleasure of our sinful life. They are masters of their souls. They have overcome the world. These people, Donatus, are the Christians – and I am one of them."[iv]

Dear Lord, I want to live so close to You that others will see Your joy in me.

WE NEED HOPE

Hope is a beautiful word. I would color it pink, or red, or purple. It doesn't carry the certainty of faith, or the assurance of trust, but it keeps us moving in the right direction. Phillips Brooks wrote, "We are haunted by an ideal life, and it is because we have within us the beginning and the possibility of it."

Hope is a march, not a dirge. It brightens gloom's corner and fills the empty void. It's a sunrise, a heartbeat, a kind word. Hope goes beyond desire and expects good. It stays around when logic fades. It meets us at wit's end corner and hails us at the crossroads of life. In death, it whispers, "Heaven is near."

History teaches us hope – Columbus's trip to the New World, the raising of the American flag on the island of Iwo Jima, the fall of the Iron Curtain. Every election, every medical breakthrough, every peace treaty offers hope.

The Bible illustrates hope. Join Anna and Simeon in the temple as they welcome Baby Jesus. Walk with the women on Easter morning as they leave the empty tomb. See, with John, a vision of things to come as he worshiped on the Isle of Patmos.

Romans reminds us to "rejoice in our sufferings, because we know that suffering produces perseverance; perseverance, character; and character, hope" (Romans 5:3-4).

The blind Fanny Crosby expressed hope so well when she wrote, "And I shall see Him face to face, And tell the story – saved by grace" (*Saved by Grace* by Fanny Crosby).

Let's join our hearts and sing along.

Dear Father, thank You for Your spark of divinity in me that gives hope in life's darkest hours. I know that You are working things out for my good. Help me to pass hope along so that it can lighten someone else's load.

GOD'S GIFT OF PEACE

Peace is sometimes an elusive kind of quality. It settles in, then takes flight when circumstances deteriorate. It's true in war, also in the hearts of human beings. Man's unrest fuels conflict.

As the disciples struggled with events leading up to the crucifixion, Jesus said to them, "Peace I leave with you; my peace I give you. I do not give to you as the world gives. Do not let your hearts be troubled and do not be afraid" (John 14:27).

I claimed this promise one dark night as I knelt by the coffee table, placed my hand on our family Bible, and quoted the verse back to God. Nothing happened at that moment; but the next day as I was washing dishes – and praying – God seemed to lower a steam shovel out of the sky and direct it toward my kitchen window. It landed in the depth of my being, yanked and pulled, until the burden lifted and peace flooded my being. I discovered that God cannot fill us with His peace when our hearts are overloaded with earthly concerns. We have to release our problems to Him and let them go.

Jesus' promise of peace is not the absence of trouble; it's letting Him enter the fiery furnace with us. Two different artists painted a picture to illustrate the concept of peace. One man painted a scene depicting a tranquil lake nestled among picturesque mountains. The other man put on his canvas a waterfall with a tree limb bending over the foam. In the fork of the branch sat a robin on its nest, soothed by the mist from the turbulent spray.

"Peace! Peace! Wonderful peace, Coming down from the Father above! Sweep over my spirit forever I pray, In fathomless billows of love" (*Wonderful Peace* by W.D. Cornell).

Dear Father, thank You for Your peace that floods my soul today. How sweet it is!

CELEBRATE LIFE

One weekend in 1983 Bob Benson, a noted writer and speaker, came to our church to share his special wit and philosophical lessons derived from everyday living. Bob was a friend from college and seminary days, so we looked forward to seeing him again.

Before the scheduled event, my husband and I took Bob to the best restaurant in our town for the evening meal. As I was walking to the salad bar, I noticed one of our parishioners eating alone in a nearby booth. I was surprised because Mrs. Rech, recently widowed, had been confined to her home with grief for several weeks.

On my way back to our table, I stopped, greeted my friend, and asked, "Are you celebrating something special today?" I thought it might be her birthday.

Mrs. Rech smiled and answered, "Yes, I'm celebrating life. I thought I had nothing to live for after my husband died. But last night, God seemed to say to me, 'You have life and you have Me, so celebrate.' I think my husband would want me to do that, too."

Later, Bob Benson recounted this episode in one of his books.

Celebrate life! I believe that's what Paul meant when he wrote that God "provides us with everything for our enjoyment" (1 Tim. 6:17b).

Look around you. What can you celebrate today? Celebrate God. Celebrate your family, your church, your friends. Celebrate the season. Celebrate the pet your children brought over because they thought you needed companionship.

I know we don't live in rose-tinted bubbles, but let's celebrate every chance we get. Invite others to join you. It's more fun that way.

Dear Jesus, help me to celebrate Your life in me in such a way that others will want to know you better.

STAND TALL

On a scale of one to ten, many senior adults would not rate high in posture. Some older ladies maintain their regal bearing, and some men have ramrod backs, but most of us shrink a little over the years. My husband and I are in that group. "Sit up straight," or "Stand tall," we sometimes say to each other as we leave for a special event.

Good posture is something we do need to practice and maintain as much as possible. It builds healthy bones, looks nice, and shows dignity. So, lets throw back our shoulders, pull in our stomachs, and walk straight.

In writing to the New Testament churches, Paul would often say, "Stand firm in the Lord" (Phil. 4:1b). Aren't you glad it's not posture or physical height, but the measure of God in us that denotes our true stature?

My mother-in-law, in her younger years, stood four feet, eleven inches tall. As arthritis took its toll, she had hip replacements, rounded shoulders, and walked with a limp. But, in my mind, she was ten feet tall. Her love for people covered her family and oozed out into the neighborhood. When she went to meet the Lord at age 91, peopled walked by her casket for three hours to say *thank you.*

So stand tall, bedridden saint.

Stand tall, wheel chair Christian.

Stand tall, you who have Parkinson's disease, or bone cancer, or back pain.

Reach beyond "What is now" to "What will be." Jesus does the measuring, and His records are always right.

Dear Father, help me to reach my full height in You as I stand on your promises and walk by faith.

BE AN OPTIMIST

Isn't it interesting that people can view things so differently? Listen to politicians as they campaign for office. Let college students and older adults discuss the same issues. Hear theologians as they lay out the tenets of their faith.

Frederick Langbridge expressed it in his poem: "Two men look through the selfsame bars; One sees the mud, the other the stars."

You've probably heard the story of the two shoe salesmen who went to scout out a new market. One man reported back, "Sorry, we can't sell any shoes here. Nobody wears them."

"Send us all the shoes you can get," the other salesman wired. "Everybody here needs them."

Pessimists see difficulties, while optimists see opportunities.

I know that life is real. Problems, frustrations, and misunderstandings bombard us daily. Sometimes they stay around and won't go away. With God's help, let's turn obstacles into steppingstones toward Christlikeness. Jesus said, "Everything is possible for him who believes" (Mark 9:23b). That's more than optimism. It's truth. Putting God into the picture changes things. It reaches out to wayward children and makes a place for retirees.

As optimism spreads, it brings in the skeptics, the procrastinator, and those wavering on the brink of decision. It fuels faith and leads Christians to action. Optimism searches for solutions and finds answers. Let's join in by bragging on Jesus, encouraging our pastor, and becoming a catalyst for good.

O God, help me to turn my negatives into positives.

STUDY SOME MORE

Five years ago I attended the 53rd reunion of my high school graduation class. As the senior class president, I was asked to emcee the event. I shared a story from American literature about Edward Bok, who moved with his parents to the United States when he was six years old and later became a well-known journalist. Bok's grandparents, and their 13 children, had transformed a desolate island into a beautiful sanctuary for birds. As each child left home, the mother admonished, "Make the world more beautiful and better because you have been in it." The challenge was handed down to grandson Edward, who built Bok Tower Gardens in Lake Wales, Florida. On several occasions, my husband and I have toured this tropical paradise and enjoyed the melodious concert of carillon bells.

To make our world better, we need to keep growing and learning. Since we rely a lot on knowledge and wisdom that has been handed down to us, reading and study is important. Good books are friends that keep us moving in the right direction

To Christians, the Book of all books is the Bible. Paul wrote to his protégé, Timothy, "Do your best to present yourself to God as one approved, a workman who does not need to be ashamed and who correctly handles the word of truth" (2 Tim. 2:15). My favorite Bibles are those I have marked (yellow for inspiration, green for promises, red for praise, and blue for passages that convict me). I am blessed to have my husband's library of commentaries and other Bible helps as I study.

As we get older, we need to keep our minds active. So read and journal. Memorize Scripture. Work your crossword and sudoku puzzles. Most of all, let God teach you new truth as you meditate on His Word. We can all do that.

Holy Spirit, thank You for being my Teacher. I have so much to learn.

Frances Simpson

SAVOR THE MOMENT

My mind is busy today. Sunday is Friend Day at church, and we have invited our new neighbors to go with us, then come to our house for dinner. Next Tuesday, we are having the retired ministers in our area over for lunch, something we do each fall. In two weeks, my brother and sister and their spouses will be here for their annual visit. So, I'm planning menus, table decorations, and time schedules.

Planning is good; it's necessary. But sometimes it robs us of today, this moment in time. The Psalmist wrote, "This is the day the Lord has made; let us rejoice and be glad in it" (Psalm 118:24). I need to work on that. "This day" is not tomorrow or next week or Christmas time.

As I look out the window above my desk, I see cloudy skies with the promise of much needed rain. I see . . . wait, let me check it out and report back to you.

Wow! It's a beautiful world out there. As I exited the back door, I saw pansies peeking from pots on the deck and mums beginning to open. Outside, I stopped to smell a gardenia bush – how fragrant! I picked a Confederate Rose to bring inside so I can watch it change from white to dark pink in one day. I heard mockingbirds talking to one another. I saw a squirrel at the top of an oak tree, looking for acorns. I observed a leaf caught in a spider web.

It's almost lunchtime. I think I'll take our sandwiches to the sunroom, and maybe my husband and I will watch it rain. Do you like tuna fish? Then pull up a chair and join us. We'll savor this moment together.

Dear Father, thank You for this moment. I rejoice in its beauty, its promise, and the assurance that You will be here tomorrow, just as You are today.

PLANT A GARDEN

Down through the years my husband and I have enjoyed gardening. Now that we are older, our gardens are getting smaller. This year we will plant tomatoes, peppers, and herbs. We are downsizing flower beds, too, substituting barrels and hanging planters that are easier to maintain.

Isaiah compared the people of God to a well-watered garden. I like that analogy. God has furnished our world with so many plants in different colors, shapes, and sizes. All of us fit in there somewhere.

We have a plaque in our garden that reads, "He who plants a garden works hand in hand with God." That's true, whether it be an outdoor garden or the inner sanctum of our heart. As we water our seed of faith with prayer, fertilize it with spending time in God's Word, and keep the weeds of doubt, envy, and pride pulled out, we can grow into the person God designed us to be.

God can change us from a thistle to a rose, from a bothersome dandelion to a much-loved orchid. He can graft us into the true Vine and make our lives a bouquet to brighten the world around us. He can use the violet of faithfulness, the snowdrop of hope, the daisy of innocence, the lily of purity, the honeysuckle of happiness, the forget-me-not of love, and the orange blossom of good will. Then we will be like a "well-watered garden, like a spring whose waters never fail" (Isaiah 58:11).

I'm glad this transformation can happen at any age – 12, 45, or 80. I've heard the testimonies.

O God, help me to "grow in the grace and knowledge of our Lord and Savior Jesus Christ" (2 Peter 3:18).

ADD SOME LAUGHTER

Would you like to belong to the Grumble Family or the Laughing Club? An anonymous author wrote: "There's a family nobody likes to meet. They live, it is said, on Complaining Street, in the City of Never-Are-Satisfied, the river of Discontent beside. And whether their station be high or humble, they are known by the name of Grumble."

If there were such a thing as a laughing club, I suppose it would include those who laugh a lot to make themselves and others feel good. If you enjoy gospel music, you may have heard George Younce sing *The Laughing Song*. His *ha, ha, ha's* always explode into laughter throughout the audience.

A growing number of health care workers are using humor and laughter to ease pain and promote healing. I saw one title in a *Reader's Digest* that claims *"Funny" Boosts Your Brain*. I'm not sure about that one.

Proverbs tells us, "A cheerful heart is good medicine" (Proverbs 17:22a). That's certainly more palatable than prescription drugs and over-the-counter medicine.

Wayne Dyer, in an article entitled *Being a Child Again*, writes, "The child in you loves to laugh. Sometimes children laugh about nothing at all, just out of sheer joy. If you're running low on laughter, try taking yourself less seriously."[v] I need to do that more.

When do you laugh the most? Much of our laughter occurs with long-time friends as we bring up stories of the past. We laugh at good jokes, questions of little children, and animals at play. Of course, it's always better to laugh at ourselves than other people. Laughter relaxes us and makes us more human. It's contagious, too.

Dear Lord, thank You for the smile in my heart that needs to erupt into laughter more often. Free me up so I can do that.

BEAR FRUIT

As Jesus closed His public ministry, he zeroed in on the role that the disciples would play in the Kingdom of God on earth. After explaining that God was the Master Gardener and that He himself was the True Vine, He stated, "This is my Father's glory, that you bear much fruit, showing yourselves to be my disciples" (John 15:8).

What kind of fruit are we to bear? In writing to the Galatians, Paul lists the fruit of the Spirit as "love, joy, peace, patience, kindness, goodness, faithfulness, gentleness and self-control" (Gal. 5:22-23). Senior adults should excel in these areas. The fruit of the Spirit does not depend on physical strength or manual labor. It is born in hearts of love as the seed of faith takes root and begins to grow.

The fruit of the Spirit pollinates to produce other Christians. In Sunday School this week, I heard an older saint tell how she introduced herself to a young boy who showed up at church one Sunday morning. Through a series of questions and answers, she discovered he was hungry. My friend took him to lunch and became Christ to him that day as she ministered to him and his family.

Christian fruit bearing brings glory to God. As family, friends, neighbors, even strangers, see the Spirit of God in us, they, too, will want to "taste and see that the Lord is good" Psalm 34:8a).

Jesus said, "every good tree bears good fruit" (Matt. 7:17a). Have you inspected your fruit lately to make sure it is mature and mellow? Does it produce a fragrant aroma? Does it lend sweetness to those around you?

O Spirit of God, cultivate my heart so that I can be a fruit-bearing Christian with enough to share with others who are hungry.

ARE YOU A SHOPPER?

Shopping sure has changed through the years. From corner grocery stores we have emerged to mega malls and super outlets. I remember when a trip to Woolworth or Kresge was like a holiday. We could buy all kinds of things with a dime. Today, both children and teens prefer game arcades and electronic stores. The price tag? More than most of us can afford.

When my husband and I were first married, we did a lot of window-shopping, which cost nothing. Later we acquired a Sear's card, which served us well in times of emergencies. Through the years we've accumulated enough "stuff" that we don't need much, so we do less shopping these days. It's still fun to walk through a nice department store or a local garden center to see what's in vogue for the season.

Through the prophet Isaiah, God called to His people, "Come, all you who are thirsty, come to the waters, and you who have no money, come, buy and eat!" (Isaiah 55:1a).

That sounds like a bargain, and I'm in the receiving line. There's no shortage of spiritual food from God's table.

To paraphrase some unknown author, "I need to go shopping. I want to exchange some self-righteousness for a supply of humility, which is less expensive and wears well. A friend showed me some pretty samples of peace, which I need to check on. I want to try to match some patience that my neighbor wears. It's so becoming to her, and, hopefully, will look well on me. I might try on that little garment of long-suffering. I never thought I wanted to wear it, but I am coming to it."

I'm glad God's supply house is well-stocked and open day or night. Let's go shopping.

Thank You, Lord, for Your open invitation to "come and dine."

WE NEED SOME RECREATION

Webster defines recreation as "refreshment of the strength and spirit." Whatever our age, we all need that. Recreation lures people to ballparks, swim clubs, and fishing holes. It brings together family and friends, even strangers. Both the seashore and the mountains beckon. Some folks take cruises and fly to exotic places. Most of us stay close to home, tend flower gardens, eat out with friends, and take an occasional trip.

At a family gathering recently, we showed slides of 35 years ago. It was fun to watch our children build snowmen, ice skate, and jump from a scaffold into deep water. The grandchildren enjoyed seeing it too.

Age and health somewhat define our recreational pursuits. Because of balance, I don't ride bicycles anymore. My golfer husband cannot hit the ball as far these days. However, there are many things we *can* do. We plan an occasional family trip and attend camp-meeting in July. We like to lunch in out-of-the-way places and walk through public flower gardens. Before winter sets in, I order some books from a Christian discount house. To cuddle up in an afghan on a cold winter evening and read is fun for us.

Paul reminds us, "whatever you do, do it all to the glory of God" (1 Cor. 10:31b). This includes recreation. We must keep time and money under God's umbrella and remember *others* as we enjoy our hobbies and times of recreation.

I've discovered that communion with God is the best renewing agent around. It can take place as we watch a sunset or fill a hummingbird feeder. The first tulip, the first robin, the first snowfall, can pull us into God's Presence and refresh our spirits so that our bodies and minds are restored.

Dear Lord, may my times of recreation and renewal magnify Your Name.

THE NAMES OF GOD

Ancient Hebrews attached great significance to names. Names identified character traits and expressed the hopes of parents for their children.

I get excited when I read about the names used to explain God. Even in Hebrew, they sound lofty and transcendent. *Elohim*, the first name God used to reveal Himself to us, is a term meaning "God of all power." As I look at the world around me and read about the immensity of space with its myriad stars and distant galaxies, I feel humbled in the presence of Elohim.

The second name God used to explain His nature is *Jehovah* or *Jahweh*, which was interpreted to Moses as *I AM WHO I AM* (Ex. 3:14a). That covers the past, the present, and the future, everything from Genesis to Revelation. I cannot fathom the scope of God's Being.

Jehovah is linked with other names to express God's faithfulness to His people. I like *Jehovah Jireh*, which means "The Lord will provide." I can testify to that.

Another term, applied to Deity, is *El Shaddai*, translated "nourisher" or "strength-giver." I'm a daily recipient of that part of God's nature, too.

The name *Adonai* surfaces at Christmas time and signifies "Lord." It draws us to the manger and helps us identify with the shepherds and Magi as they worshiped Jesus.

Each of us has our favorite names for God. I like *Father, Creator, The Alpha and Omega*. When I think of Jesus, I pray *Savior, Prince of Peace, Master.* To the Holy Spirit, I offer *Comforter, Helper, Teacher.*

O God, I approach your throne today with awe and wonder. With Isaiah, I cry, "Holy, holy, holy is the Lord Almighty; the whole earth is full of his glory" (Isaiah 6:3).

HEAVEN IS MY HOME

One hot July afternoon, when I was ten years old, I fell asleep on the couch and dreamed that Jesus was descending to earth with a cloud of angels and people were rising to meet Him in the air. Our family arrived at heaven's gate, where Saint Peter greeted us and asked to see our tickets. We stated that we did not know we needed tickets. I awoke with a start and hurried to find mother so I could tell her my dream.

Earlier in the week, I had walked down the street to a tent revival meeting being held in our neighborhood. The evangelist had preached on heaven. "If I could talk to the preacher, I know he could tell me how to get tickets," I said to mother. Mother didn't think it was a good idea, so I went outside to play instead.

One year later I knelt at an altar of prayer and accepted Christ as my Savior. That day I received my prized ticket to heaven.

I am reading *Heaven Your Real Home* by Joni Eareckson Tader. I'm a fast reader so I barged through several chapters, then stopped and started over. It was not the material so much that drew me; it was the descriptive words and phrases, the stellar analogies, the way the author pulls the reader into the very vestibule of heaven.

I can't picture heaven as much as I can feel it. Streets of gold and gates of pearl pale in the light of God's all-consuming Presence. Someday, I plan to join the great multitude shouting, "Hallelujah! Salvation and glory and power belong to our God" (Rev. 19:1b).

Yes, heaven is my home, and I've started packing. See you there.

Dear Jesus, my human mind cannot grasp the beauty, the scope, the majesty of heaven, but my spirit is reaching out to embrace it. Thank You for the pull that gets stronger each day.

Subtracting

When I was a child,
I talked like a child,
I thought like a child,
I reasoned like a child.
When I became a man,
I put childish ways behind me.

1 Corinthians 13:11

SAYING GOOD-BYE

Saying *good-bye* is sometimes hard. I watched a set of grandparents say good-bye to their son, daughter-in-law, and three grandchildren as they left for the mission field. I will never forget the expression on their faces, nor the tears that filled their eyes as they gazed through the airport window and waved goodbye. Missionaries, evangelists, and military personnel are my heroes when it comes to saying good-bye.

As a minister's wife, I've shared some good-byes, too. In a farewell letter to one congregation, I wrote: "You have been our family. Many miles separate us from parents, relatives, and hometown friends. Thank you for understanding and including us in your circle of love and concern."

Charles Hastings Smith, evangelist and poet laureate of Arkansas, wrote in his poetic style, "Every week, somewhere, some place, I say 'good-bye' to someone and my heart always twinges and another piece of me is left behind."[vi] In our mobile society, good-byes sometimes outnumber the hellos.

After being with His disciples for three years, Jesus told them He was going back to His Father's house: "Do not let your hearts be troubled . . . In my Father's house are many rooms . . . I am going there to prepare a place for you. And if I go and prepare a place for you, I will come back and take you to be with me that you also may be where I am" (John 14:1-3). Aren't you glad for that promise?

There will be no good-byes in heaven. The rafters will ring with hellos as we greet loved ones and settle in for eternity. I want to see Jesus. I'll look up Peter, James, and John and say hello to Mary Magdalene. Perhaps you and I can take a walk together.

Dear Jesus, thank You for coming to where I am so that I can be with You forever.

DO YOU EVER FEEL LONELY?

The theme of a popular Gospel song several years ago states that after we accept Christ as Savior, we will never be lonely again. I don't believe that is scriptural. I know that Jesus is a friend for all seasons and that the Holy Spirit is our Comforter; it's the word never that rings untrue. Sometimes, I get lonely to see our son Mark and his family, who live nine hundred miles away. I miss Florida's beaches, Indiana's covered bridges, Kansas' sunsets, and Ohio's farmland – places we have lived and raised our families.

I believe Jesus was lonely in the Garden of Gethsemane as His disciples slept while He prayed. I think He expressed loneliness when He cried from the cross, "My God, my God, why have you forsaken me?" (Mark 15:34b). Jesus understands our lonely times.

The death of a spouse has been rated the greatest stress factor in the life of any senior adult. The long nights, meal times, trips to the store, church, all become reminders of the missing loved one.

Solitude, however, need not equate sadness. It can draw us into God's inner circle as we depend on Him more. I have a dear friend, Myrtle, who lost her husband about ten years ago. They had no children, so Myrtle lives alone, using a cane and a walker to get around. By calling on the telephone and sending notes, she has become a caregiver for her church and community. If something needs to be done, call Myrtle, and she will find someone to do it. No wonder Myrtle has such an upbeat spirit.

Jesus promised, "And surely I am with you always, to the very end of the age" (Matt. 28:20b). So when the road gets lonely, take Jesus' Hand and keep walking.

Dear Father, were you lonesome that first Christmas night? Thank You for being with me in my lonely moments.

HEALTH IS RELATIVE

Old age is not the common denominator for illness. The young and the in-between get sick too. Sometimes, they die. Nevertheless, bodies do eventually wear out, and many senior adults have health concerns. Read your church prayer list and join in the conversations around you. You will find that doctor visits and lab tests take a toll on both time and money.

My husband had aggressive cancer seven years ago. So we understand chemotherapy, radiation, blood therapy and all that goes with it. Today he is cancer free. However, some folks we know have not had a remission. God loves them too.

Our goal, as older adults, is to stay as healthy as we can. Most illnesses can be maintained. Thank the Lord for doctors and nurses who help, for research that finds new treatments, and for medication that alleviates pain and promotes healing. We should do our part, too. The need for proper diet, exercise, and rest blares at us from many angles.

Have you heard these quips? Old age is when:

- Everything hurts, and what doesn't hurt doesn't work.
- You get winded playing checkers.
- Your back goes out more often than you do.
- You sink your teeth into a steak and they stay there.

The Psalmist declared, "For you (God) created my inmost being; you knit me together in my mother's womb" (Psalm 139:13). Surely God, who made us, understands the aging process too.

O God, You who know every bone, every muscle, every organ in my body, thank You for the built-in healing process that takes place daily.

WHAT'S YOUR SLEEP INDEX?

Do you get enough sleep? Sometimes – you say. Well, I'm in that group, too. Research tells us that people have more trouble sleeping after age 65. They tend to get sleepy earlier in the evening and wake up earlier in the morning. That's okay, if we can adjust our schedules accordingly. Some people do all right with five or six hours of sleep, while others need at least seven or eight.

One thing for sure, insomnia is not fun. Many things can cause it – an overactive mind, chronic pain, lack of exercise, stress, too much caffeine. Pick up most any magazine and you will find an article on how to get more sleep. Try whatever seems good to you; it just might help.

Evidently, King David was having sleep problems when he wrote, "On my bed I remember you; I think of you through the watches of the night" (Psalm 64:6). As someone said, "When you can't sleep, don't count sheep. Talk to the shepherd."

The Apostle Paul listed sleepless nights along with the other hardships he endured.

My saintly mother-in-law struggled with pain from arthritis for many years and often did not fall asleep until three or four in the morning. By her bedside, lay her Bible and hymnbook, sources of strength during those night hours.

I don't want to be like the sluggard in Proverbs, who slept himself into poverty (Proverbs 6:10-11), nor like the five foolish virgins who slept when they should have been buying oil (Matt. 25:7-8). I do, however, treasure a good night's sleep.

Whatever our sleep index may be, whether we are lying down at night or getting up in the morning, God is with us. I think I need a nap – Z-z-z-z.

Thank You, Father, for restful sleep. It's so refreshing.

FORGETFULNESS IS CONTAGIOUS

I admire people who can easily recall names, numbers, and important trivia. They have a knack for connecting with people and making them feel at home. I am not one of those persons. Even after trying word association and forming mental images, I still fall short.

I have read that, after 20, there is a gradual decline in the ability to remember. We also know that disease can ravage smart people's brains and do double take with memory. Most of us fall somewhere in the middle and need to work at recalling information.

My husband and I are partners in this endeavor. Without belittling one another, we probe each other's minds until one of us will usually come up with the name or the data we are seeking. I am learning to do the alphabet thing – go through the letters until one triggers a response. Sometimes it works.

You've probably heard the joke about the minister who asked an old-timer, "Do you spend much time wondering about the hereafter?"

The old-timer replied, "I'll say! Whenever I find myself in front of the refrigerator with the door open, I have to ask myself, "What am I here after?"

These days, that's not an unusual scenario for me. If I linger long enough or return to the task at hand, usually the answer comes.

Hebrews reminds us, "And do not forget to do good and to share with others, for with such sacrifices God is pleased" (Hebrews 13:16). The world needs senior adults, mature in faith, and so in tune with God that the important things in life are forever fixed. Let's make a list of these things now so we'll not forget them tomorrow.

Dear Father, teach me how to expand my memory capacity. Help me to be patient with others who need help too.

ACCIDENTS DO HAPPEN

Eight weeks ago, as my husband and I were coming home from church, the driver of another car ran a stop sign and slammed into the side of our vehicle. We were not seriously injured, but we did experience some pain and anxiety. It took seven weeks to get our car repaired.

Though vehicle accidents are the most common cause of accidental death, the home seems to be the most dangerous place for the elderly. Many falls take place while people go about their everyday activities. For those over 74, falls often result in a fracture of the spine, hipbone, or wrist. I'm in that age group, so I need to take notice.

To prevent falls, we should have our vision and hearing checked regularly, exercise as much as we can, rise slowly, and select proper footwear. We may have to rearrange furniture, get rid of scatter rugs, and put night lights throughout the house. We need to install grab handles and nonstick mats in bathrooms, avoid ladders, and be careful going up and down stairs.

I like the benediction in Jude, verse 24: "To him who is able to keep you from falling and to present you before his glorious presence without fault and with great joy."

This Scripture does not refer to physical falls, but to spiritual setbacks, which are even worse. As Christians, we need to remove any attitudes, doubts, or sins that might cause us to stumble. If, perchance, we do fall, we must ask forgiveness, get up, and start moving again. Prayer and Bible reading will strengthen our spiritual muscles and help us walk better. Remember, the Great Physician is always on call.

O Holy Spirit, thank You for guiding me along the pathway of life. Help me to avoid any pitfalls that would hinder my walk with God.

THE WAITING ROOM

Many of us spend quite a bit of time in a waiting room somewhere. My husband and I keep a stack of appointments on the kitchen counter including visits to our primary physicians, our dentist, the dermatologist, the audiologist, and the oncologist. Taken together, they represent a lot of waiting.

All kinds of things can happen in a waiting room. Ila, a member of our Sunday School class, recently shared a prayer request about a lady she had met in the waiting room of the hospital where she volunteers. My friend approached the lady, who was alone, and asked if she needed help. In the course of the conversation, the lady stated, "I've been praying for a friend to come into my life."

"You've just met her," Ila stated in her characteristic style.

In waiting rooms, pastors pray with parishioners. Family members hold hands and weep quietly. Sometimes reconciliation takes place and resolutions are made. Change can take place in the waiting rooms of our lives.

The Psalmist wrote, "Wait for the Lord; be strong and take heart and wait for the Lord" (Psalm 27:14).

Job waited for the Lord mid suffering and abandonment. Moses waited on the back side of the desert until his time arrived. John waited on a lonely island until God opened heaven and let him see inside.

Where is your waiting room? Is it your home? The place where you work? Your church? God is already there; look for Him.

O God, in the waiting rooms of my life, help me to remember that you are always on schedule.

HOSPITAL RUNS

After awaking at 2:00 in the morning with a heavy pain in my chest and extreme nausea, I agreed with my husband that I should go to the emergency room at our local hospital. After eliminating a possible heart attack, the doctor made his diagnosis – gallstones. I had surgery several days later, and the problem was solved.

Thank the Lord for hospitals, doctors, nurses, lab technicians, and all the other medical personnel needed to diagnose and treat illness. It's a team effort, including the patient and his or her family. When my husband was undergoing chemotherapy, we were given a medical booklet explaining how a caring support group greatly enhances a cancer patient's recovery and helps promote healing. That's true for other illnesses too.

In a way, the church is like a hospital or clinic where people come with all kinds of problems. Broken families and sin-sick prodigals enter our doors. Some are bound by addictions and cry "Help," as they pass through. Others are simply looking for answers and a better quality of life.

Jesus said, "It is not the healthy who need a doctor, but the sick . . . For I have not come to call the righteous, but sinners" (Matt. 9:12-13). So, if we are to be a part of God's intensive care unit, we must introduce people to Christ, the Great Physician, who can heal both soul and body.

Is your church a healing center where anyone – yes, anyone – can come for an extreme makeover? Do you have some interns around who are willing to get their hands dirty by getting involved in the healing process? Do you have a support group ready to encourage and give some booster shots along the way? Are you on the team? If not, join today.

Oh, God, use me in your healing ministry.

Frances Simpson

NOSTALGIA

Nostalgia is a kind of homesickness that slips in unannounced and pops up occasionally like a jack-in-the-box. It's not depression or melancholia; it's a pleasant memory that wants to stay awhile.

Nostalgia hides in vacant bedrooms and sits at the kitchen table. He joins us as we make cookies and homemade ice cream. He helps carve the turkey at Thanksgiving, sits atop the Christmas tree, bursts from an Easter egg. He peeps from the back seat as we leave for vacation. He runs along the beach and skips along mountain trails.

Nostalgia blows in when autumn arrives, raps on the window when snow falls, plays on the ceiling when the fire burns low, walks amid tulips in the spring, rides on the moon, and slides down the rainbow. He sits by me in church and kneels when I pray. He tiptoes when I'm sick and claps when I laugh.

The Psalmist often expressed his homesickness for God: "My soul yearns, even faints, for the courts of the Lord; my heart and my flesh cry out for the living God" (Psalm 84:2). Do you remember times when God came near and wrapped His cloak of love around you? Have you felt His enabling power as you accepted a new assignment? Do you recall revivals, Sunday School contests, dinner-on-the-ground? What about the special people, now in heaven, who have enriched your life through the years?

Nostalgia has a way of resurrecting the past and helping us to sift through the present in order to make tomorrow better. So, welcome the warm feelings and gentle reminders, but don't let them stay around too long. Today is the first day of the rest of our lives. We still have things to do, places to go, friends to meet. That, too, is part of growing older.

Dear Lord, thank You for the special times that make life good.

PRAYER CHANGES ME

Did you ever have a plaque in your home that read, "Prayer changes things"? We did. In answer to prayer, I've seen God change people, alter situations, and stretch resources. I've been there when hopeless situations evolved into life-changing events – not immediately always, but in God's time.

One of the greatest miracles for me is how God can change my heart, my attitude, and my perspective so that He can use me for His purposes. Often, as I pray about a delicate situation, the Holy Spirit begins to probe: *Do you know all the facts? Did you speak unkindly? What have you done to rectify the situation?*

Time and again, after wrestling with God, I come away changed. God can help us love the unlovely, turn the other cheek, go the second mile. He not only helps us to see other people as He sees them, but He shows us how we look, too. As we wait before a holy God, we become more like Him. Problems seem to grow smaller, burdens lift, and we forge ahead stronger and better than we were before.

Jesus said to His disciples, "Therefore, if you are offering your gift at the altar and there remember that your brother has something against you . . . First go and be reconciled to your brother; then come and offer your gift" (Matt. 5:23-24).

Do you need to visit someone today, make a telephone call, or write a letter? I've done it often and always feel better.

E. Stanley Jones, the Methodist missionary, wrote, "Prayer is our channel of openness to His channel of fullness so we can become His channel of blessing."

Dear Lord, You, who have forgiven me so much, help me to pave the way for reconciliation when it is needed. Remind me that others may be hurting more than I am.

STAY FOCUSED

As I'm getting older, I have a harder time staying focused, especially on busy days. I sometimes start several jobs at one time and fail to get them all done by the end of the day. I'm sure I would be more relaxed if I finished each task on schedule and left some less important things undone. This is something I need to work on.

Last Christmas, our family gave my husband and me a digital camera. I don't know a lot about photography, but I do understand that focus is important. Focusing determines whether your subject will appear sharp or blurred in the picture. The instruction booklet points out that proper focusing depends on distance, lighting, balance, and keeping the camera level. The subject should appear in the viewfinder at the exact moment that we snap the picture

The writer of Hebrews tells us to "fix our eyes on Jesus, the author and perfecter of our faith" (Hebrews 12:2a). Focusing on Jesus doesn't happen automatically. We need to study our Manual, the Bible, and zoom in so we can get a clear picture of God and what it means to be made in His image. As much as possible, we should keep proper balance in our lives and stay level headed when the world around us is topsy-turvy.

Jesus is the focal point of the Bible. The Old Testament points to His coming and tells how God prepared a people to receive Him. The New Testament announces His arrival, then chronicles His words, deeds, miracles, and teachings so that we will understand God better. As a pastor, my husband had the words, "Sir, we would like see Jesus" (John 12:21b) displayed on the pulpit where only he could see them. Yes, we need to focus on Jesus, the Light of the World.

I exalt Thee, O Lord!

HOUSEKEEPING

My husband and I enjoy a clean house. Both of us pick up after ourselves quite well, and I make sure things are in order before I go to bed each night. When I was younger, I did my weekly housecleaning on Friday. Now, because of age and energy level, I divide it into daily tasks. Instead of spring and fall cleaning, I do a yearly cleaning, beginning in January and taking one room at a time until the job is done. Yes, it takes several months.

Claudia Allen Rowe, a staff writer for *The Charlotte Observer*, wrote: "Cobwebs hang like bad-housekeeping banners in the corners. Toys dot the landscape. Newspapers crowd the hearth. The kitchen sink overflows with last night's dishes. It's the Saturday morning jungle. And then, the door bell rings."

Cobwebs are so flimsy that they often go unnoticed until the light hits them a certain way. We might compare a cobweb to something that hampers or entangles us, perhaps without us being aware of it. It might be a little thing in the beginning but keeps growing until we are trapped by it. Only the light of the Holy Spirit shining in our lives can bring these cobwebs into the open and help us deal with them.

Jesus said to the Pharisees, "First clean the inside of the cup and dish, and then the outside also will be clean" (Matt. 23:26). This kind of housekeeping is a full time job.

My friend, Dr. Fletcher Spruce, wrote: "Look into your heart. Let God's broom of great love sweep its corners clean of hate, pride, prejudice, doubt, fear, lust, and greed. Make room for love, humility, tolerance, patience, courage, hope and faith."[vii]

Search me, O God, and know my heart today. Try me, O Savior; know my thoughts, I pray. See if there be some wicked way in me; Cleanse me from ev'ry sin, and set me free (*Cleanse Me* by J. Edwin Orr).

Frances Simpson

DOWNSIZING

Many older adults find that they need to downsize at some point. We have friends who recently moved from a large house to a patio home, which was quite traumatic for them. We downsized to one car a couple of years ago, which took some adjustment. As we get older, we downsize Christmas decorations, gardens, and shopping trips. We don't seem to need as many things in our latter years; or, at least, we can't take care of them.

People downsize more than possessions. My husband doesn't play golf much these days. I don't make cinnamon rolls as often. We don't travel like we used to. There are exceptions, of course, but most of us find that some things change as we get older.

Even in church work and volunteerism, we may notice a difference. For many years I taught an adult Sunday School class and wrote curriculum materials. One Sunday, two years ago, as I struggled with insomnia at 4:00 in the morning, the Lord seemed to say, "It's okay. You can resign as teacher of the Friendship Sunday School class." Today, my husband and I are still members of that class, serving as greeters and doing what we can to help our energetic teacher.

Sometimes, because of age, we need to resign boards, committees, and community work. Younger people are waiting to take our places. We need to boost them, pray for them, and not get in the way of progress.

Though we may need to downsize possessions and activities, our spirits can soar as we enlarge our capacity for worship and adoration of God. Let's read it again: "Trust in the Lord with all your heart and lean not on your own understanding; in all your ways acknowledge him, and he will make your paths straight" (Proverbs 3:5-6).

Dear Lord, help me to hold on to the best while releasing some of the good.

HOW IS YOUR HEARING?

One-third of people over age 65 have some hearing loss. You may be in that number. I remember seven summers ago when, over a period of two weeks, my husband lost all hearing in his left ear. When hearing in the right ear started going down rapidly, his doctors were baffled and assumed he would be totally deaf in a few days. I remember the night I cried out, "O God, I want to be able to talk to my husband." With lots of prayer and a new doctor, his hearing in the right ear stabilized at forty per cent. With a hearing aid, he does quite well.

What sounds do you enjoy hearing – the voices of your grandchildren, beautiful music, a mountain stream, night sounds, table conversation, your pastor's sermon? I enjoy hearing the birds singing in the morning and the laughter of little children. Hearing is God's great gift to us; let's not take it for granted.

God sent the prophet Isaiah to preach to a people who were "ever hearing, but never understanding" (Isaiah 6:9). I don't want to be in that crowd.

To those who questioned His teachings, Jesus said, "He who belongs to God hears what God says. The reason you do not hear is that you do not belong to God" (John 8:47).

Wow! That's close preaching. I've read the communication tips for those who have physical hearing problems: face the person to whom you are speaking; stay within a few feet; talk on a one-to-one basis; reduce the background noise, if possible. Perhaps, as Christians, we can get some cues from this list. When we talk to God, we need to focus on Him and Him alone. Let's stay as close as we can and block out the distractions that clog up our spiritual hearing. Then listen . . . really listen.

"*Speak, Lord, for your servant hears . . .*" (1 Samuel 3:9, NKJV).

Frances Simpson

EYE TROUBLE

When I daydream, I like to think of one of my favorite places, put myself in the picture, and then relax. I usually find the beach in Pompano Beach, Florida, one mile from where we lived for eleven years. I watch the waves rush in, push my toes in the sand, and gaze at cumulous clouds as they float across the sky. Then I transport myself to Wichita, Kansas, to see the sun set across the lake in front of our house. I usually end up in my own back yard in Charlotte, North Carolina. How great is the gift of sight!

As we get older, our vision tends to change. Usually, we learn to adjust by wearing glasses or contact lenses. Some people have glaucoma, cataracts, macular degeneration, or other problems that need medication or surgery.

When Jesus was on earth, he healed many who were blind. Remember blind Bartimaeus, who cried, "Have mercy on me," as Jesus passed through Jericho (Mark 10:47)? How do you think the world looked to Bartimaeus the day he was healed?

It's a cliché, but one of the greatest problems people of all ages have is "I" trouble. Paul wrote to the church at Corinth, "The god of this age has blinded the minds of unbelievers, so that they cannot see the light of the gospel of the glory of Christ" (2 Cor. 4:4). As senior adults, we need to make sure our spiritual eyes are centered on Christ.

I like Eugene Peterson's rendition in *THE MESSAGE* of 1 Corinthians 13:12):

"We don't yet see things clearly. We're squinting in a fog, peering through a mist. But it won't be long before the weather clears and the sun shines bright! We'll see it all then, see it all as clearly, as God sees us, knowing him directly just as he knows us." That's better than 20/20 vision.

Dear Heavenly Father, help me to clear my vision so I can see you better.

WHAT ABOUT ELECTRONICS?

I'm not good with electronics. Neither is my husband. Resetting the clocks after a power outage is a major ordeal. I need step-by-step instructions to play our stereo system or use the digital camera.

It seems that gadgets and appliances used to be simpler to operate. Just turn the "on" knob and adjust the volume – but then they didn't give the same job performance either.

I can't imagine going back to a manual typewriter after using a word processor or sweltering under a handheld fan while others enjoy air conditioning. I love my push button vacuum and my self-cleaning oven.

About eight years ago when my word processor died, my family insisted that I get a computer that would do the same thing plus lots of other good "stuff." I debated, prayed, and scanned the newspaper ads. When a big sale came up, I plunged in. From the beginning, my prayer has been, "Lord help me use this computer for your glory."

I took a few classes, had a little one-on-one help, asked my grandchildren lots of questions, and now I belong to the group with fast access, e-mail capability, and research unlimited. However, I find the grandchildren have far outmaneuvered me with their web sites, I-pods, and electronic games.

Actually, we should not be surprised at the vast knowledge of our day. God made us in His image and told us to take charge. The problem is, human beings often try to work without God. Proverbs tells us, "The fear of the Lord is the beginning of knowledge" (Proverbs 1:7a). I wish everyone knew that.

Dear Lord, help me to keep learning as I throw the net out a little farther. Thank you for those brave souls who help me along the way.

WHEN THE ANSWER IS NO

Small children ask a lot of questions – May I have a cookie? Can I go outside? Will you play a game with me? Many times the questions are legitimate; but timing, safety, and priorities come into play. Children don't understand that sometimes "No" is for their own good.

That's true throughout life, especially as we get older. "No, I'm sorry, but you cannot drive the car anymore," my brother tried to explain to my mother after she experienced several mini strokes. She didn't like it, but she had to abide by the rule.

"No, you cannot eat sweets," the doctor tells his diabetic patients. Some may disobey the directive, but usually there are consequences.

We ask God for many things, knowing that He hears and answers prayer. God said to Jeremiah (and us): "Call to me and I will answer you and tell you great and unsearchable things you do not know" (Jer. 33:3). I'm thankful for God's Yeses. I have some miracle stories I could tell you – one is the salvation of my Father ten months before he died.

Sometimes, God says, "Wait." When the answer finally comes, we understand the reason for the delay.

At other times, God says, "No." The Apostle Paul wrote about a thorn in the flesh that he repeatedly asked God to remove. In the end, Paul testified, "I will boast all the more gladly about my weaknesses, so that Christ's power may rest on me" (2 Cor. 12:9b).

Some unknown soldier wrote, "I asked God for strength that I might achieve; I was made weak, that I might learn humbly to obey. I asked for health, that I might do greater things; I was given infirmity that I might do better things."

Dear Father, thank You for hearing my prayers and then doing what is best for me.

TAKE A DEEP BREATH

Do you ever feel as if you are not getting enough oxygen into your lungs? I do. Occasionally, I will hyperventilate, which means I breathe too fast. As people get older, they sometimes forget to breathe properly. Colds, pneumonia, or exhaustion can interrupt the flow of air, too.

The respiratory center in our brain stem controls our breathing. During the process, the blood takes up oxygen and dispenses carbon dioxide. Both of these functions are important. Ordinarily, we do not make a conscious effort to inhale and exhale air; it's an involuntary action. However, the depth and rate of breathing can be altered. Exercise increases the breathing rate. Sleep and rest lowers it. When breathing becomes too irregular, a person may experience chest pain, weakness, or fainting.

This is a good analogy for healthy Christian living. As we inhale (take in) the Spirit of God, love, faith, peace, and other virtues flow through our spiritual veins. At the same time, we need to exhale (get ride of) fear, doubt, resentment, and other things that hinder Christian growth.

I've seen spiritual hyperventilation as people feverishly do the work of the church without the help of the Holy Spirit. Jesus said, "The Spirit gives life" (John 6:63a). Without God's enabling power, we become anemic Christians and accomplish little for God's kingdom.

The Hebrew word for God's Spirit is *rauch*, which means moving air or wind. Dan Boone wrote, "The Holy Spirit is the moving, empowering, life-giving, evil-cleansing, hope-promising, heart-activating breath of God."[viii]

Holy Spirit, breathe on me.

NIGHT VISION

My husband likes to tell the grandchildren about the time when he was eight years old and went to bed, near an open window, to awake during the night and see a ghost fluttering over his bed. Too frightened to make a sound, he lay there until his ghost turned into a white window curtain buffeted by the night breeze. Things look different at night. Behind every shrub is a would-be robber; airplanes become UFO's; a twig turns into a snake ready to strike.

I remember a poignant illustration given by C.S. Cowles in a Sunday School lesson several years ago as he wrote about his first "night walk" in Yosemite National Park. After some instructions by the guide, all flashlights were switched off at 10:00, and darkness took over. Everyone quickly gathered around the ranger for security.

As the group stood quietly for a few minutes, a miracle happened. People began to get their "night eyes," just as the guide had promised. An eerie glow filled the darkness, illuminating trees and rocks along the forest path. A mystical feeling of joy surged through the crowd.

The Psalmist wrote, "weeping may remain for a night, but rejoicing comes in the morning" (Psalm 30:5b). Have you ever had a dark night of the soul when it seemed even God had abandoned you? In your darkest hours, stop and take another look. Whether you see Him or not, Jesus stands at your bedside of pain and suffering.

Turn to the last book of the Bible and read about John's vision of heaven. He writes, "there will be no night there" (Rev. 21:25b). Aren't you glad?

O God, thank you for speaking to me in the night hours. Your Presence holds me steady until dawn pushes the darkness away.

SECOND CHANCES

Jesus told a story about a young man who claimed his inheritance and headed for a far country so that he could eat, drink, and be merry. After a while, he ended up in a pig pin, feeding hogs. There, the young man came to his senses and headed home – not to be a son, but a servant in his Father's house.

You know the rest of the story – how the son arrived home to find a loving, compassionate father waiting for his return. As the son confessed and repented, the servants outfitted him with new clothes and shoes. The family ring was placed on his finger. "Let's have a feast and celebrate," said the Father. "For this son of mine was dead and is alive again; he was lost and is found" (Luke 15:24a).

I met an eighty-two-year-old prodigal not long ago. For years, he had ordered church folks off his property when they came to visit his bed-ridden spouse. So, after the man's wife died, the congregation was surprised to see him in church one Sunday morning. Several of us invited him to our Sunday School class, and he began to attend. Over the next few weeks, I watched as the man's countenance softened; sometimes tears would surface. One afternoon my husband visited our new friend and presented the Gospel to him. That day, as heaven rejoiced, another prodigal came home.

Many second chances and new beginnings dot the crossroads of our lives. This doesn't mean that God is a namby-pamby, or that he looks the other way when we do wrong. It does speak of God's love that reaches out to the sinner and stays around when everyone else leaves. David wrote, "As a father has compassion on his children, so the Lord has compassion on those who fear him" (Psalm 103:13).

Dear Father, thank You for not giving up on me and my loved ones.

KEEP THE LINES OPEN

Ring-g-g-g.

Every morning at 9:00, our daughter, Karen, phones to check on my husband and me. Our son, Mark, who lives 900 miles away, calls regularly, too, as do siblings and special friends. Keeping connected is a gift we sometimes take for granted.

Communication has certainly changed through the years. The wireless telegraph, developed by Guglielmo Marco in 1895, ushered in radio and television. Alexander Graham Bell's telephone has changed from a big box on the wall to a small hand-held device transmitting, not only voices, but pictures and text, as well. Today, with satellites and computer technology, voices bounce around the world.

Occasionally, I will pick up our phone to find that the dial tone is dead – the result of a broken line somewhere or a blown transformer. To keep my track phone operational, I must keep the battery charged. Sometimes, an e-mail is returned because an address is unknown .

How is your prayer line working? Is it up to date? Is your spiritual battery charged? Does worldly debris clog the line somewhere? Jesus told His disciples to "always pray and not give up" (Luke 18:1b). That's a good formula for any age, but it does take work.

As I lay awake last night doing some personal inventory at the beginning of a new year, I did a repair job. I asked God to help me realign some priorities. I repented of eating too many sweets and calories over the Christmas season. I vowed to make Sundays more holy. So, today, I open the door to a new year and say, "Welcome! I'm ready."

Good morning, Lord. Thank You for helping me clear the line so I can hear you better.

I DON'T UNDERSTAND, LORD

We live in an explosive age of information and cybernetics (the dispensing of that information). Scientists are discovering new galaxies, researchers are isolating more genes, and computers contain more data. Using *Google Earth*, I can travel around the world via satellite.

In the midst of this vast information, questions remain. Why do good people suffer? Why do tsunamis, earthquakes, and tornados work havoc around the world? Why does God allow terrorists, arsonists, and sex offenders to do their dirty work?

Job, in his suffering, questioned God, too. In essence, he cried, "Where are you?"

After listening to Job's complaints, God asked Job some questions: "Where were you when I laid the earth's foundations?" "Do you know the laws of the heavens?" "Will the one who contends with the Almighty correct him?" (Job 38:4, 33, 40:2).

In the end, Job replied to the Lord, "I know that you can do all things . . . things too wonderful for me to know" (Job 42:2-3).

Do you ever have questions? I do. Many times I have knelt and cried, "I don't understand, Lord. Where are you in all this?"

At age 75, I still don't have all the answers, but I've decided to major on the things I do know. I know today that God is Creator of all things, that He loves me, and sent His Son to be my Savior. I know that my sins are forgiven and that I'm ready for heaven. I know that God showers me daily with blessing after blessing.

That's enough for now; but the moment I cross heaven's threshold, I will understand what Charles Tindley meant when he wrote, "We will understand it better by and by."

Dear Father, thank You for your patience with me in these days.

SELF-CONTROL

Self-control is listed last in the fruit of the Spirit (Galations 5:22-23), but we cannot relegate it to the sidelines. It may not claim top billing with love, joy, and peace, but it is still an important virtue in the Christian life. In fact, all the other fruit depend, in part, on how we practice self-control.

Paul wrote, "But I discipline my body and bring it into subjection, lest, when I have preached to others, I myself should become disqualified" (1 Cor. 9:27, NKJV).

It's not the big no-no's that bother Christians. It's letting the legitimate, everyday affairs of life get out of control until they hamper our effectiveness and put us on the defensive – things like overloaded schedules, watching too much television, putting off until tomorrow what we should do today.

One of my weaknesses is warm cookies, straight from the oven. "How many did you eat?" my husband always asks as he walks by.

"Too many," I answer.

Paul Harvey, the news commentator, stated, "What a tragedy that man should conquer outer space and fail to conquer his inner space."

Discipline or self-control helps to keep us healthy in body, mind, and spirit. As we practice rules of good health and guard our minds from the evil around us, things just go better. Let's control our tongues too. Some oldster prayed, "Keep me from the fatal habit of thinking I must say something on every subject and on every occasion."

Do you need more self-control? I do. Let's pray together.

O God, I offer to you my body as a living sacrifice. I want to be holy and pleasing to you at all times (Romans 12:1).

STRENGTH FOR TODAY

My husband and I have a difficult time, these days, opening jars and packaged goods. Last week, I enlisted our ten-year-old grandson to help me open a jar of applesauce. To retrieve pills from their bubble compartment takes major effort. Most senior adults find that their physical strength is not what it used to be.

About a year ago I ordered the *MAYO CLINIC FAMILY HEALTH BOOK*, which says to move, move, move. Most people my age don't move fast, so I was glad to read that moderate physical activity, on a regular basis, gives most of the same benefits as rigorous exercise. My husband and I do not have a workout program, but we do maintain our house and yard, which helps to keep us moving. I walk a mile with a neighbor about four days a week. My husband has his own walking routine using his homemade shepherd's stick. We both do stretching exercises for specific ailments and endeavor to keep our energy level up. Is this enough? I hope so.

Even as I write this, I think of my friends who are on walkers, in wheelchairs, and often confined to bed. Oh, how they would like to take a step without pain, or reach into the refrigerator to get a jar of mustard. Doctors and physical therapists give routines and medicines to help movement and flexibility, but sometimes they are limited.

Even as our physical strength wanes, moral strength and fortitude can remain firm. Spiritual stamina can increase as we exercise our faith muscles, stretch our vision, and walk daily with the Lord.

"The Lord is my strength and my shield," wrote the Psalmist (Psalm 28:7a). Let's say "Amen" to that.

Thank You, Lord, for strength for this day.

LEARN CONTENTMENT

The Apostle Paul declared, "I have learned the secret of being content in any and every situation" (Phil. 4:12b). I'd like to talk to this man who was buffeted by the storms of life and took it all in stride.

The writer to the Hebrews stated, "be content with what you have" (Heb. 13:5). I understand that better. I know that money, houses, and gadgets do not bring happiness and fulfillment. However, I still get frustrated when plans go awry, when I don't seem to have enough time or energy, or when people I love get into trouble.

"I have learned," Paul says. That must be the key. Paul probably did not go around searching for contentment. It must have emerged from God's cache of grace as he traveled around Palestine, Asia Minor, and Rome under divine assignment. It stayed during shipwreck, prison stints, beatings, and church problems. For Paul, contentment was active, not passive.

Contentment is not lounging around in mediocrity or declining an opportunity to improve a situation. It's realism – seeing life as it is – and then feeling at home in God's presence. Even though a person may be alone or in a care facility, contentment can settle in like leaves on an autumn day. I've witnessed it in the lives of folks I know.

Reinhold Niebuhr, a leading Protestant theologian, wrote: *O God, Give us serenity to accept what cannot be changed, courage to change what should be changed, and wisdom to distinguish the one from the other.*

Only God could help a crusader like Paul find contentment in the controversies of life. He can help us, too.

O God, help me to struggle less and rest in You more.

OVERCOMING THE GIANTS

What word would you use to describe your Christian life? Is it a joyful, exciting, fulfilling journey? Or might it be challenging, even lonely and difficult at times? Perhaps, it's all of the above. The word that I use most often is overcoming. Overcoming doesn't sound glamorous, but it does spell victory.

In Numbers 13, Moses sent twelve men to spy out the land of Canaan. All twelve brought back glowing reports. Ten said, "We can't go in; too many giants live there." Joshua and Caleb countered, "With God's help, we can possess the land."

Overcoming means there are some giants around. It is a process that takes work. But, as the Israelites found out, the result is worth the effort.

Jesus said, "In this world you will have trouble. But take heart! I have overcome the world" (John 16:33b). How? By depending on the Father, doing good, praying for His enemies, and forgiving those who wronged Him.

Do you have any giants in your life? Usually, different age groups have different giants. For senior adults, they may be illness, loneliness, financial need, or immobility.

Have you heard these complaints?

Your knees buckle and your belt won't.

You know all the answers, but nobody asks the questions.

You sit in the rocking chair and can't get going.

Your little black book contains only names ending with M.D.

Overcoming denotes action. Let's roll up our sleeves and slay the giants in our lives by claiming God's Promises and proving them true.

O God, thank You for the shield of faith that helps me face my giants with confidence.

Multiplying

May God Almighty bless you,

And make you fruitful and

multiply you . . .

Genesis 28:3 (NKJV)

LIVE ALLYOUR LIFE

I read an intriguing article by Morris Chalfant entitled "I Hope You Live All Your Life," in which he stated, "Some are very old at 35 because they feel they have nothing to give to life. Others continue to be extremely productive because they believe they have a contribution to make."[ix]

I smiled at the author's suggestion that those who want to know what it feels like to be old should smear dirt on their glasses, stuff cotton in their ears, put on heavy shoes that are too big, and wear gloves; then try to spend the day in a normal way. It might be funny, if it were not so true. Some of us are part way there.

Most of the senior adults I know live active lives – going and coming, involved with family, volunteering in churches, hospitals, schools, and nursing homes. I've heard them say, "I don't know how I ever had time to work at a regular job."

However, there does come a time when we have to slow down and live on a different plane. Illness, pain, immobility, loss of hearing or sight can complicate life and cause people to retreat into themselves. It's then that we need to stop feeling our own pulse long enough to look at the needs around us.

Are there some children next door who need a substitute grandma or grandpa? Why not invite someone over for coffee and dessert? Maybe you could teach a granddaughter how to knit or crochet. Grandpas are good at sharing gardening tips. It doesn't take much energy to make telephone calls, write notes, and send e-mails.

The Psalmist wrote, "The righteous . . . will still bear fruit in old age" (Psalm 92:12-14a). Retirement might be our most productive time. Are you ready?

Dear God, show me what You want me to do today.

FRIENDS ARE FOREVER

I like *ideals* publications with their beautiful pictures, easy reading poetry, and hometown articles. I have several displayed on our coffee table where my husband and I can pick them up often and reminisce.

I looked through my stack of *ideals* recently and found four on *friendship*. As I scanned them, friendship took on many faces. In childhood, friendship was for playing tag, skipping rope, shooting marbles, and sledding down a snow-covered hill. In adolescence, it changed to sleepovers, fishing trysts, ball games, trips to the corner drug store. Adults enjoyed picnics in the park, quilting bees, county fairs, and revival meetings. Some things have changed, but friends still enjoy getting together.

Friendship is a gift we give ourselves. Sometimes it's a diamond in the rough, something that we have to polish until it becomes a precious gem. True friendship takes time and effort, but once established, it lasts forever. My husband and a college friend, who lives 900 miles away, talk on the phone at least once a month. They still have news to share, questions to ask, plans to make. Get together with an old friend, and time seems to evaporate.

I like the statement made by some anonymous writer, "I love you not only for what you are, but for what I am when I am with you."

Jesus said to His disciples, "Greater love has no one than this, that he lay down his life for his friends" (John 15:13). A few days later He died on the cross for the sins of the world.

"What a Friend we have in Jesus, All our sins and griefs to bear!" (Joseph M. Scriven).

Thank You, Lord, for being my all-time friend.

LOVE YOUR ENEMY

In many parts of the word today Christians are being persecuted for their faith. It's an age-old plot. Evil doesn't mix with good. It lashes out at God like the serpent in the Garden of Eden and stays around to make life difficult.

Jesus said to his disciples, "Love your enemies and pray for those who persecute you" (Matt. 5:44). Not many senior adults will admit to having avowed enemies, but we can probably name a few people who complicate life for us. Even in our free society there are those who try to demoralize Christians and make them run for cover.

A recent *Family Circus* cartoon showed Jeffrey, wearing boxing gloves, standing outside P.J.'s closed door and complaining to his mom that P.J. wouldn't come out to play. Have you ever not wanted to play by someone else's rules because it always spelled trouble?

Jesus taught us to handle our enemies with love, prayer, forgiveness, and good deeds. That's a tough assignment and may not remove all the hurt and pain, but it does fit us for heaven and helps us to witness to others along the way.

I read about a lady who moved to a new neighborhood and was warned that a gang of boys was trespassing on people's lawns. The lady, a great lover of flowers, invited the boys in for milk and cookies and they ended up helping her plant and weed her garden.

Paul Martin, a well-known evangelist, preached in our church many times. I'll never forget a statement he made about what to do when people throw stones at you. "Have the liniment ready," he said. "Someone may hurt an arm and need help."

Dear Lord, help me to make my enemy my friend.

BRIDGE BUILDING

Several years ago our family vacationed together in Northern Michigan. We had gone there when our children, Mark and Karen, were small and they wanted to introduce their children to the area. It was fun to meld three generations as we recalled old memories and made some new ones.

One day we rode the ferry to beautiful Mackinac Island in Lake Huron. No automobiles are allowed, so we explored the island in a horse-drawn buggy. Another day we rode across Mighty Mac, the five-mile bridge spanning the Straits of Mackinac. I later read how David Steinman, son of a factory worker, designed and supervised the construction of the bridge, which others said was impossible.

Allen Dromgoogle wrote a beautiful poem about an old man who, after crossing a deep chasm, stopped at the close of day to build a bridge across it. When a bystander asked, "Why?" he replied, "There is a young man not far behind me. I am building the bridge for him."

On the cross, Christ made a bridge between sinful man and a holy God. The Bible talks about other bridge builders: John the Baptist paved the way for Jesus; Andrew brought his brother to meet the Messiah; Barnabas introduced Paul to the Christian Church. Missionaries, teachers, writers, and parents are all bridge builders.

Senior adults, in tune with God, are good at building bridges between family members, disgruntled neighbors, and church cliques. Christian maturity has an audience.

God said to the prophet Ezekiel, "I looked for a man among them, who would . . . stand before me in the gap" (Ezek. 22:30a). Might you be that man or that woman?

O Lord, help me to bridge some troubled waters in the lives of people I know.

Frances Simpson

WHAT DO YOU HAVE TO GIVE?

A few weeks ago our pastor gave a moving illustration about Vedran Smailovic, a cello player for the Sarajevo Opera Orchestra. *The New York Times* magazine, in July 1992, printed a photo of Mr. Smailovic sitting in the middle of the street in front of a burned out bakery, playing his cello. Twenty-two people had been killed there. So, for 22 days, Smailovic braved artillery fire to sit in the ruins and play. Some people thought he was crazy, but he did what he could – speak softly with his cello, one note at a time.

Mr. Smailovic gave his music; Michelangelo gave his paintings; Helen Steiner Rice gave her poems. To fulfill God's assignment, Moses used a rod, David used a slingshot, Paul used a pen. God has a way of taking what we give to Him and multiplying it to help a needy world.

Senior adults still have a lot to give. Because of better health, higher education, and the need for something meaningful to do, the number of people 75 and older with jobs is increasing. I saw a cartoon recently that said, "God put me on earth to accomplish a certain number of things. Right now I am so far behind I will never die." Sometimes I feel that way.

What do you like to do? Do you enjoy cooking, sewing, gardening, working on cars, or making crafts? Do you play an instrument or sing? Do you like to work with children, teen-agers, or shut-ins? Do you like office work, planning social events, making flyers, or decorating bulletin boards? As you list the things you like to do, you will discover what you have to give? Paul reminds us, "God loves a cheerful giver" (2 Cor. 9:7b). So, volunteer with a smile.

Dear Father, thank you for being such a giving God. Help me as I do what I can.

BE A GOOD LISTENER

Listening is an art. It takes practice to be a good listener – to note facial expressions, catch the reflections in the voice, honor pauses, and read between the lines without interrupting. Good counselors listen more than they speak. It's interesting how talking about a problem often formulates its own answer.

A group of children was asked, "What's special about your grandma?" Their answers tell us something.

"Grandmas listen when no one else will."

"Grandmas are the best at keeping secrets."

"Grandmas are really truly interested in your dead frog."

I'm a multi-task person. That's not good when it comes to listening. I have to work at it – whether it's listening to my husband's commentary on the morning news, answering a telephone call, or absorbing the sermon on Sunday morning. Some folks have a hard time listening because they are formulating their own speech on the subject. They may even interrupt to have their say.

I have in my files a prayer for the aged that says, "Lord, keep me from the habit of thinking that I must say something about everything."

An Old Testament song extends a beautiful invitation, "Come and listen, all you who fear God; let me tell you what he has done for me" (Psalm 66:16). Senior adults have amassed a lot of knowledge, wisdom, and experiences that need to be shared with the next generation. But, as we do so, let's make it short and sweet. The Holy Spirit will talk for us.

Dear Father, help me to hold my tongue when I should be listening.

Frances Simpson

THE GIFT OF HOSPITALITY

My husband and I have eaten in many lovely homes and elegant restaurants, but my most memorable dinner took place at a group home where one of our church members lived. (I'll call him Jim.) When Jim found out that our family would be moving to a new assignment, he was devastated.

Early one morning the resident counselor at Jim's home called to invite our family to dinner on Friday night. I was surprised but responded, "Sure, we would love to come."

When we arrived at the house, a maitre – de, with towel draped across his arm, bowed and invited us in. Our friend, Jim, brought a bowl of M & M's for our 'hors-d'oeuvres. Another host gave us a tour of the house, including the kitchen where the men were preparing the food. I was amazed how well the counselor had prepared the residents for dinner guests.

Words cannot describe my emotions that evening as my husband carved the meat, the men brought the food in, my husband said grace, we passed the food, and ate. A lot of indelible memories are etched on my mind.

After dinner, Jim gathered everyone in a circle and prayed for our family. I think God smiled as He looked down on the scene – seven children in men's bodies and their guests.

Do you have the gift of hospitality? It's listed in Romans 12 along with prophesying, teaching, and giving (v. 13). So it must be important. Jesus told us to invite "the poor, the crippled, the blind and the lame" (Luke 14:21b). Could that be the neighbor across the street that speaks a different language, the lonely widows in our church, a child who needs a grandparent? Invite someone over. Both you and your guest will feel better.

Dear Lord, help me to make our home a place where folks want to come.

GRATITUDE SHOWS

Jesus traveled throughout Palestine teaching, healing the sick, forgiving sins, casting out demons, feeding the people, and raising the dead. I wonder how many took time to say "Thank You"?

Some did show their gratitude – the woman who anointed Jesus' feet with expensive ointment was saying "Thank You." The demon-possessed man from Gadara wanted to follow Jesus after his miraculous deliverance. The writers of the Gospels and the Apostle Paul lavished praise on the Only Begotten Son of God.

What about us? We, too, come asking. Our church prayer chain is filled with requests for healing, jobs, the salvation of loved ones, and other concerns. When God answers, do we say, "Thank You"? Gratitude is a lifestyle. It's like a soft blanket that settles in around us and keeps us warm. Paul wrote that Christians should overflow with thankfulness (Col. 2:6). Are we part of the "overflow" crowd? Someone looking on may see the difference and join in.

The renown Passion Play, observed every ten years in the village of Oberammergau, Germany, began in 1633 as a *thank you* to God. In the surrounding villages two-thirds of the people had died from the plague sweeping across Europe. During a special prayer meeting, called by the village priest, a young girl suggested that one year in ten be set aside to reenact the passion of Christ as an act of praise to God. Not another death was caused by the plague in Oberammergau.

A grateful heart knows that the "Lord is good and his love endures forever" (Psalm 100:5a). What is your gratitude rating? Maybe we all need to raise it up a notch.

"*I will praise you, O Lord my God, with all my heart*" (Psalm 86:12a).

ENJOY HOLIDAYS

Many of our happiest memories center on the holidays that dot our calendars. Special days have a way of wrapping themselves around us and tying family and friends together with warm feelings and forever moments.

One of my hobbies across the years has been collecting traditions, activities, and ideas for celebrating these special days. I've scoured bookstores, searched magazines, quizzed people, and observed others in their times of Christian celebration. About five years ago I compiled these ideas into a book for our family and had a local office supply store print it. On the front is a picture taken at our 50th wedding anniversary. Throughout the book are photographs taken at Christmas, birthdays, graduations, vacations, and other special occasions. To introduce each of the days, I penned a meditation, many of them featuring family members.

The Old Testament records several festivals and holidays observed by the Jewish people as they came together to worship and celebrate their religious heritage. I'm sure the Hebrew children looked forward to the Feast of Tabernacles each fall when they lived with their parents in booths made from leafy branches for seven days. What stories they must have told as they remembered God's goodness to the nation of Israel.

The Bible exhorts, "Rejoice in the Lord always. I will say it again: Rejoice!" (Phil. 4:4). Observing holidays and special occasions gives us many opportunities to do that as we share our faith with those around us and pass it on to the next generation. So, put out your crèche at Christmas time, make your thanksgiving list, hang a flag, give an Easter basket. Family members and neighbors will help you. Together, let's celebrate.

Dear Father, thank You for the joy of living life in partnership with You.

LET'S HAVE A PICNIC

It was raining Friday evening, but my husband suggested that we have a picnic.

"Where?" I asked.

"In the family room," he replied.

We set up our game table and two folding chairs, closed the drapes, and ate our picnic fare of hot dogs, potato salad, and baked beans. As we laughed and ate together, I began to feel warm on the inside. I remembered other picnics – on the beach in Florida, on the patio in Indiana, on the back porch in Kansas, at Mount Gilead State Park in Ohio. Joy welled up as I remembered God's goodness down through the years.

I'm sure Jesus and his disciples enjoyed many picnics as they traveled the roads of Palestine and took boat rides on Lake Gennesaret. The Gospel writers tell how Jesus used a boy's lunch to turn a remote countryside into a picnic ground. I enjoy reading about the early morning breakfast on the shore of the Sea of Tiberias, where Jesus fed seven discouraged disciples and taught them a lesson on feeding sheep.

Have you ever wandered in a wilderness, hungry and thirsty – not for physical nourishment, perhaps, but for the *Living Water* and *Bread of Life* that Jesus offers? Jesus declared, "I am the bread of life. He who comes to me will never go hungry, and he who believes in me will never be thirsty" (John 6:35).

Are you in a barren land today? Look around. You may see an oasis ahead, or someone may show up with some loaves and fish. Do you have something that God can break, bless and use to help someone else? If so, give it to Him and get ready for a picnic. You might even have some leftovers.

O Lord, thank You for meeting me in the deserts of my life.

BOOSTER SHOTS

When our son Mark was five years old, I announced to him at the breakfast table one morning that it would soon be time for his booster shot.

"Why, Mom?" He asked. "Is it booster season?"

It was a logical question since Mark had already experienced measles, mumps, and chickenpox, illnesses that seemed to come at certain times of the year.

I'm not sure what I answered as I stifled a smile, but I should have said, "Yes, Mark, it's always booster season." As Christians, we should regularly administer morale builders and offer spiritual tonics.

A neighbor, who is in law-enforcement, stopped recently to check on my husband and me after someone tried to break into our house. What a blessing it was to have Mike take our hands and pray for us before he left.

I recall the hand written note on a card I received during one difficult time. My friend wrote, "Remember, this is no surprise to God. He is already working on it." Wow! That's a faith builder.

In grocery stores I often engage crying toddlers in conversation so their mothers can shop in peace. I've played games with restless youngsters in a doctor's office or on an airplane. It's fun to give simple compliments to clerks, waitresses, and handymen. A smile and a "thank you" go a long way.

In writing to the early church, Paul stated, "My purpose is that they may be encouraged in heart" (Col. 2:2a). Do you know someone who needs a booster shot? Make a list of things you can do this week and have fun.

Dear Lord, use me to lighten someone else's load.

WHO ARE YOUR HEROES?

Our lists of heroes have a way of changing through the years. A toddler chooses mom and dad (hopefully, they stay on the list). Older children may branch out to grandparents and teachers, even Superman. Teens make their list of Who's Who often with a slant toward the rich and famous. College students and adults sometimes end up with a smorgasbord as they look for someone to follow.

But, as a mature senior adult, who are your heroes? I sat down this week to make a list of my own special people and find it is too long to navigate. Rev. Michaels, my first pastor, jumps out, along with lay men and women in that church who helped me grow from a babe in Christ to a young pastor's wife. I remember those in our five pastorates who went the second mile to minister to our family and help us fulfill God's assignment in that place.

My list of heroes includes missionaries like Elizabeth Cole, who spent years in an African leper colony; and Mary Scott, who went from missionary, to prisoner, to the head of a great missions organization. I stand at attention when I read about Wycliffe Bible Translators and JAARS Inc, the organization that provides transportation and technical support services to make translation in remote areas possible.

At the top of your list, and mine, reigns Jesus, who left heaven's glory to die on the cross for the sins of the world. According to Hebrews, "Jesus lives forever, he has a permanent priesthood. Therefore he is able to save completely those who come to God through him, because he always lives to intercede for them" (Hebrews 7:24-25).

Jesus is not a long-ago hero, but a here-and-now Savior.

"*Wonderful Savior, wonderful Savior, Thou art so near, so precious to me*" (*Wonderful Savior* by J.M. Harris).

LOOK FOR HIDDEN TREASURE

Have you ever gone on a treasure hunt? Some adventuresome souls dive for gold at the bottom of the ocean or join an archeological expedition. Most of us limit our treasure hunts to games played with planted objects and maps telling us how to get there first.

If we really started looking for treasure, we'd find all kinds of riches, not hidden, but ignored or taken for granted. Perhaps you have read the story of Ali Hafed, who sold his farm and went looking for diamonds so he could be rich. He died, still looking. The man who purchased Ali Hafed's farm later discovered acres of diamonds. You know the moral of the story.

In my husband's desk, along with important papers, lies one of his treasures – a small gift-wrapped box with a note from our six-year-old grandson, which says, "I took an ordinary box as empty as can be. I filled it with a special gift and wrapped it carefully. But please don't ever open it. Just leave the ribbon tied. Hold it tightly near your heart because my love for you is inside."

I'm sure you have your own treasure box with pictures and priceless mementos – baby booties, homemade cards, thank you notes, certificates, rocks, and shells. Each item tells a story you want to remember.

"The house of the righteous contains great treasure," reads Proverbs 15:6. The writer must refer to faith, hope, and love; to forgiveness and second chances. Certainly, he includes nature and all its bounty. Ultimately, he must be talking about heaven.

Yes, God has provided a treasure house of righteousness, and the Bible is our roadmap for finding it.

Dear Father, how manifold are your blessings! Thank you.

YOU CAN MAKE A DIFFERENCE

Several years ago I received a starfish pin along with the story about a man who was walking along the beach picking up starfish and throwing them back into the sea. A young man watching him asked, "Why are you throwing starfish back into the ocean? There are miles and miles of beach. You can't possibly make a difference."

The man threw another starfish and replied, "It made a difference to that one."

There are many worthy causes bouncing around the world that will make a difference in the lives of people. Feeding hungry children, building houses for homeless families, and taking the Gospel to those who don't know about Christ are on the list.

I read a "good news" article in our newspaper this morning about a woman who is making a difference in the lives of children touched by disaster. Kathryn Martin, whose two-year-old son was killed in a tornado in 2005, has become the driving force behind a good-will bus, stocked with toys, games, coloring books, and a television set. Volunteers take the bus to storm damaged areas around the country to help keep children busy and happy while their parents reassemble their lives. Thank the Lord for people who make a difference in our world.

Jesus said to His disciples, "And if anyone gives even a cup of cold water to one of these little ones because he is my disciple, I tell you the truth, he will certainly not lose his reward" (Matt. 10:42).

What can you and I do to make a difference in the lives of others? Can we tutor a child in reading? Carry dinner to the family of a sick mother? Work in the church nursery? Visit the nursing home nearby? There is so much to be done. Do you want to help?

O God, use me for your honor and glory. Where do you want me to start?

Frances Simpson

THE CHRISTIAN'S BUILDING CODE

I am nestled in an armchair, snug and warm, while a winter storm rages on the outside. The howling winds chase each other around the corners of the house. They push against the doors, dance wildly on the branches of the trees, then race helter-skelter across the lawn.

Inside my house, I feel secure. The strong bricks and insulated glass have been tested in other storms. I know they will stand.

I have witnessed other kinds of storms as they beat upon homes and families, people I know and love. Winds of misfortune, icy relationships, waves of sickness, the chill of death take their toll. I've watched some homes break under the onslaught – shattering families, hurting children, destroying dreams. Others come through wiser and strong, their faces etched with understanding; their words resounding with compassion; kindness, the keynote of their lives.

What makes the difference? Jesus began a parable by saying, "Therefore everyone who hears these words of mine and puts them into practice is like a wise man who built his house on the rock" (Matt. 7:24). The Rock? David sang about Him: "My God is my rock, in whom I take refuge" (2 Sam. 22:3a).

No matter how broad our rock foundation may be, the walls of our spiritual fortress must go high in order to stand the storms of life. Use the building blocks of Bible study, prayer, church attendance, and witnessing. Cement them together with the fruit of the Spirit. Then you can sing with another hymn writer, "On Christ, the solid Rock, I stand; All other ground is sinking sand" (*The Solid Rock* by Edward Mote).

O Lord, be the Superintendent of my building project.

SING PRAISES

Nothing draws us into God's presence like music, whether it be a praise chorus, a Fannie Crosby hymn, or Martin Luther's *A Mighty Fortress Is Our God.* Even Queen Victoria could not remain seated as she heard the magnificent *Hallelujah Chorus* for the first time. Music has been rightly called the language of the soul.

What's your favorite hymn? Some fanciful soul composed the following list:

The Dentist's Hymn: *Crown Him With Many Crowns*

Golfer's Hymn: *There is a Green Hill Far Away*

The Politician's Hymn: *Standing on the Promises*

Optometrist's Hymn: *Open My Eyes That I Might See*

Chuckle, then turn to Acts, Chapter 16, verse 25 and read, "About midnight Paul and Silas were praying and singing hymns to God, and the other prisoners were listening to them." Not all singing takes place in church. It reverberates through hospital rooms, nursing homes, and jail cells. Usually, someone else is listening.

I like to read stories behind the writing of great hymns. One that stirs me deeply is that of Horatio Spafford, a prosperous attorney and businessman, who became a modern day Job. A son died of scarlet fever; the great Chicago fire of 1871 wiped out his real estate holdings; like Job, he was erroneously censored for "unconfessed sin"; his four daughters were killed in a shipwreck. Later, in the very place where the ship sank, Spafford went to his cabin and penned *It Is Well with My Soul.*

Do you like that song? I do. Let's sing the chorus together – Yes, out loud. What part do you want to sing? I believe God will hear our harmony and smile.

Dear Lord, thank You for music that calls me to worship.

BUILD AN ALTAR

Altars are an important part of Old Testament history. Noah built an altar when he and his family exited the ark. Abraham built an altar when he arrived in the land of Canaan. Jacob, while fleeing for his life, stopped long enough to meet God in a dream and build an altar. Altars were places where God met man.

As the Hebrew nation developed around corporate worship, altars were built in the tabernacle, then the temple. There, priests offered sacrifices for the sins of the people: pointing to the time when Christ, the Lamb of God, would die for the sins of the world.

"We have an altar," the writer of Hebrews states (Heb. 13:10a).

The first congregation my husband pastored worshipped in a small army barracks building with a homemade bench for an altar. Many times I met God in that place. Later, we had churches with elaborate altars and cushioned kneeling pads – always, they were places of forgiveness, healing and reconciliation. Against the backdrop of the altar, people join the church, say their wedding vows, dedicate their children, bury their dead. The altar is a sacred place, a holy place.

Do you have a special place where you like to meet God? My first personal altar was under a big oak tree in our backyard, where I would slip out at night and talk to God about my teenage problems. Through the years I have enjoyed kneeling at the altar in empty sanctuaries to pray. Nowadays a rocker often becomes my altar or a chair on our back deck. Maybe you like a front porch swing where you can pray for your neighbors as they pass by.

Altars pull us into God's presence; when we leave, His presence goes with us.

Take my life and let it be consecrated, Lord, to Thee (Frances Havergal).

TAKE COURAGE

The word courage brings to mind all kinds of scenes with heroes and dangerous missions. We see them on our television screens and read about them in our newspapers – stories of policemen and firemen who die in the line of duty, inner-city teachers who defy ignorance, and missionaries who serve in gospel-resistant countries.

The Bible abounds with stories of courageous men and women who put their lives on the line to challenge the enemies of God. Look at Daniel, thrown in the lion's den for refusing to bow down and worship the king. Consider David, who met Goliath with a slingshot and faith in Israel's God. Watch Esther as she goes before King Xerxes to plead for her people. Follow Paul on his missionary journeys and sit with John on the Isle of Patmos. Talk about courage – those who follow God need it at every turn of the road.

One stormy night Jesus walked on the water to his frightened disciples, saying, "Take courage! It is I. Don't be afraid" (Matt. 14:27). Oh, how I like that verse!

Raymond Lindquist wrote, "Courage is the power to let go of the familiar." Senior adults understand that. It takes courage to face change with dignity and an open mind. My husband has a brother who is selling his house so he can go into an assisted living community. That's not easy at 86 years of age. It takes courage.

Facing illness and death takes courage. When my father was in the throes of cancer, I sent him a little poem that read: "*Every morning lean thine arms upon the window-sill of heaven and gaze upon thy Lord; Then, with the vision in thy heart, turn strong to meet the day.*" When my father died, I found the poem in his Bible. I thank the Lord for this anonymous poet who gave my Father courage in his last days.

O God, give me courage to meet the challenges that come my way.

KEEP TRYING

If at first you don't succeed, try, try again, says an old adage. Most toddlers fall the first time they try to walk. Those who hit the most home runs, sometimes strike out. In the beginning most novelists receive rejection slips. R. H. Macy failed seven times before his New York department store caught on. Have you read Abraham Lincoln's list of failures before he became President of the United States? I can't make a pound cake like my mother-in-law, but I'm still trying. An Air Force motto states, "The difficult we do immediately; the impossible takes a little longer."

The Psalmist wrote: "Commit your way to the Lord; trust in him and he will do this: He will make your righteousness shine like the dawn, the justice of your cause like the noonday sun" (Psalm 37:5-6). Worthy causes begin with God, but commitment and determination help bring them to pass. Leonardo Da Vinci wrote, "O Lord, Thou givest us everything at the price of an effort."

I enjoyed reading an article in the February 2008 *Reader's Digest* about Alfredo, an illegal immigrant, who came to a farm in central California to pick tomatoes. He worked hard, acquired new skills, went to night school, and eventually graduated from Harvard Medical School. Today, he specializes in a high-tech form of brain surgery.

What do you want to do for the rest of your life? You really aren't too old to try something new. Maybe God is already suggesting a thing or two. According to a message published in *The Wall Street Journal*, "Don't worry about failure. Worry about the chances you miss when you don't even try." Why not make a "to do" list, then pray about it? God may be looking for someone just like you.

O Lord, help me not to be afraid to try something new for you.

THE POWER OF WORDS

I am an avid reader. I like descriptive words and phrases that paint pictures in my mind and help me see with the eyes of the soul. I have two "time out" chairs. One is a rocker in my bedroom. Beside it, I have three different Bibles (I like to compare verses), a textbook on theology, and a devotional book on Psalms by Don Wyrtzen. On the table by my chair in the living room, I have a cookbook from the 1920's, a book on prophecy, Joni Eareckson Tada's book on heaven, a devotional book featuring the poetry of Helen Steiner Rice, and an inspirational novel.

I don't read a lot of cartoons or comic strips, but I do enjoy *Family Circle* and *Pickles*. Both of them involve three generational families. The writer of *Family Circle* depicts childhood in whimsical fashion using naïve statements and cute questions, the kind of things we wish we had written down when our children were small.

Pickles, on the other hand, portrays retirement life in slow moving episodes, using both words and silence to explain the logic and foibles of old age. I enjoy *Pickles* because I live there.

No matter what age we are, words are important. They can build up or tear down. They can encourage or disillusion. They can present the Gospel of Christ or become the Devil's workshop. The Apostle Paul wrote, "Do not let any unwholesome talk come out of your mouths, but only what is helpful for building others up according to their needs, that it may benefit those who listen" Eph. 4:29).

Let's keep our words sweet; we may have to eat them someday.

"*May the words of my mouth and the meditation of my heart be pleasing in your sight, O Lord, my Rock and my Redeemer*" (Psalm 19:14).

DO YOU DREAM A LOT?

A dream is defined as an experience that a person lives through during sleep. Some are pleasant; others, not so pleasant. I usually end up lost somewhere or teaching a class to find that my notes are gone. I'm always glad to wake up and find myself at home in bed. I wouldn't want to be psychoanalyzed at that point.

WEBSTER'S DICTIONARY identifies a dreamer as a visionary. Peter told the crowd at Pentecost that when God pours out His Spirit, "young men will see visions, your old men will dream dreams" (Acts 2:17b). I think the two may overlap a bit.

My husband and I don't do a lot of teaching these days. We greet and play hostess instead. But at church yesterday our youth president asked us if we would teach a membership class for about 20 teenagers. *Teenagers? We are in our late 70's* – No, I didn't say that, but I did think it. The President's reasoning was that our long tenure in the church qualified us for the assignment. I hope that's the case.

Anyway, as I thought about our teen group and scanned the material, my mind shifted into high gear and I started dreaming. You see, I joined the church when I was 11 years old and feel some identity with teenagers, especially those from unchurched homes. What if we could present the mission of the church in such a way that these kids would want to be a part of it? What if those who did not know Christ could be brought to Him in a soul-winning session? What if, on Easter Sunday, ten new members could be welcomed into our local church?

What if's? – do you have some floating around? Maybe it's time we put handles on them and pull them within reach. I believe the Lord will help us do that.

O God, give me strength equal to my dreams.

KEEP THE RIGHT PERSPECTIVE

Someone sent me a beautiful story on the Internet about a little girl who was walking home from school one day when an electrical storm quickly developed. The mother, concerned that her daughter would be frightened, got in her car and drove slowly along the route from school looking for her. Soon she spotted her daughter and pulled to the side of the road to wait. Suddenly a streak of lightning split the sky followed by a roar of thunder – then another, and another. At each flash of lightning, the child would stop, look up, and smile.

The mother hurried her daughter into the car and asked, "What were you doing?"

The child answered, "God just keeps taking pictures of me."

I know the story is illogical, but it does remind me that in the storms of life – storms that I have no control over – God's Word will be "a lamp to my feet and a light for my path" (Psalm 119:105). Jesus knows the road that I'm taking and will meet me at every danger point along the way.

This week we had 24 continuous hours of intercessory prayer and Bible reading in our local church. As I was reading aloud from Psalms, I realized that David had a lot of problems. We do too. We get sick; loved ones die; budgets fall short. We are not always applauded when we go the second mile. Like Elijah, we feel alone sometimes.

A missionary was returning home on board the same ship as a famous celebrity. As the ship docked, a band played and flags waved – not for the missionary but for the celebrity. Later that night the missionary, alone in his room, questioned God, like David did.

"Remember, son," God whispered. "You are not home yet."

Dear Lord, thank You for helping me to see You in the middle of my storms.

LIST MAKING

A few days ago my husband looked through the stack of notes on the kitchen counter and suggested, "Maybe you should write an article on list making." Though I knew he was being a bit catty, I followed his advice.

I've always been a list maker. Now that I'm getting older, the need for reminders has accelerated. I have a calendar on my desk that records important dates and appointments, but my husband and I need daily hands-on recall. So, in one pile I have doctor, dentist, optometrist, audiologist, and oncologist appointments; in another one, I have miscellaneous items. Often I make daily lists of things to do and places to go. If I have guests for dinner, I usually make an hour-by-hour list.

Lists are important. The cook prepares her menus and makes her grocery list. The gardener studies the seed catalogue, then makes his list. The builder studies his blueprint and makes a list of materials to buy. Lists help us to operate at maximum capacity.

Lists can enhance our times of worship, too. Make a list of your favorite Bible verses and memorize some. Write down your favorite Bible characters. How are they alike? How are they different? When you have a hard time falling to sleep, make a thanks list starting with A and going through the alphabet. Mine usually begins like this: A is for angels; B is for the Bible; C is for Christ. Why don't you make your own list and I'll finish mine?

James reminds us that we should not get so busy with our lists that we leave God out of our plans: "Instead, you ought to say, 'If it is the Lord's will, we will live and do this or that'" (James 4:15). Ouch!

O God, thank You for the constant reminders that you are in control.

THE BIG GAME

Sports occupy center stage for some people, whether the games are on television, in a nearby sports arena, or a high school gymnasium. As we get older, most of us become spectators more than participants. We enjoy watching our grandchildren play ball, run relays, and take part in competitive swimming. Senior adults are usually better at water aerobics, golf, shuffleboard and other games that require less strength and mobility.

I've observed some fundamental principles that apply to athletes and their games. First of all, every team has a coach to train, challenge, and direct the players. Much depends on the ability and communication skills of the coach. Ask my grandsons and they will tell you the best coaches around.

Good athletes train hard. They learn discipline and know how to work together in order to win the game. Their close-knit huddles and hand-slapping congratulations promote unity. If one player gets a home run or a touchdown, the whole team cheers.

As Christians, we are in a big race. The writer of Hebrews talks about it: "Therefore, since we are surrounded by such a great cloud of witnesses, let us throw off everything that hinders and the sin that so easily entangles, and let us run with perseverance the race marked out for us" (Heb. 12:1).

We qualify for the Christian race when we accept Christ as Savior. The Bible is our Rulebook. Our Coach is God, the Holy Spirit, Who calls the moves and guides us on the playing field. Our trophy will be the crown of life which God promises to all those who cross the finish line. What a victory celebration that will be!

Holy Spirit, thank You for teaching me the rules of the Christian race and helping me to live by them.

Frances Simpson

PATRIOTISM IS STILL IN STYLE

Patriotism is still in style. It's a mixture of national pride and gratitude – proud to be a citizen of one's country and grateful for the freedom and opportunities it offers. For many of us, religious freedom tops the list. We may argue with it at times, but thank the Lord it's still there.

Mature adults know that freedom carries responsibility. It's not a matter of either-or, like flipping a coin. Rightly understood, it is the balance beam that holds society and families together.

As Christians, one of our responsibilities is to pray for those in authority (1 Tim. 2:1-2). To be the leader of a nation, an institution, a company, or a church is to carry the weight of that organization on one's shoulder. This gets heavy at times. Look at the face of a president on the day he is inaugurated and four years later when decisions hang heavy and public acclaim is not what it used to be.

We need to respect our president, our pastor, our parents, those who stand in lines of authority. We should pray daily for God's leadership in their lives, and ours. In our peopled world lines of authority have a way of intersecting each other with one cause resting on another. We are not always sure where we fit in. That's why we need to pray.

My country – yes, my country! I can vote and even run for office. I can express my dissatisfaction, write my congressman, and consider both sides of an issue. So wave your flags, enjoy the fireworks, and sing the national anthem. It's all part of keeping patriotism in style.

"*Long may our land be bright with freedom's holy light; Protect us by Thy might, Great God, our King!*"(*My Country 'Tis of Thee* by Samuel F. Smith).

SHAKE HANDS WITH NATURE

David sang to the Lord, "When I consider your heavens, the work of your fingers, the moon and the stars, which you have set in place, what is man that you are mindful of him, the son of man that you care for him?" (Psalm 8:3-4).

Let's join David as he shakes hands with nature. Smile at the morning sun. Let the wind run its fingers through your hair. Wave to the branches as they bend their greeting. Smell the perfume-laden air. No fashion show ever displayed more scintillating colors than nature's garment. No symphony can match its music. It's God's way of saying, "Good morning, my child."

It's true that we worship the Creator, not the created, but God's handiwork has a way of pulling us into His presence. Nature's many moods are the language of artists, poets, and songwriters. Newman Flower wrote, "I believe in the God of my garden, the God of the trees . . . The God of the Light . . . The God of the Night."[x]

The world around us teaches so much about God – a God of all power and all knowledge; a God who loves color and harmony; a God of variety, Who creates giant redwoods, yet splatters the desert with scrub pine.

From nature's bounty come fruits and vegetables, another gift from God. Why not plant a garden? If you can't do that, try a container of herbs. My favorites are parsley, chives, peppermint, and basil. In the fall I dry the leaves in the microwave and place them in jars for the winter.

Maltie D. Babcock wrote, "This is my Father's world . . . His hand the wonders wrought." Let's all say, "Amen."

"*O Lord, our Lord, how majestic is your name in all the earth!*" (Psalm 8:9).

BIRDWATCHING

Jesus, the Master Teacher, had no chalkboards, overhead projectors, or power point equipment to enhance the things he said. Instead, He used the canopy of heaven and its furnishings to illustrate His teachings. He talked about grass and flowers, seedtime and harvest, light and darkness . . . and birds. I think Jesus liked birds.

To a crowd that had gathered on a hillside in Galilee, Jesus said, "Therefore I tell you, do not worry . . . Look at the birds of the air; they do not sow or reap or store away in barns, and yet your heavenly Father feeds them. Are you not much more valuable than they?" (Matt. 6:25-26).

Several days ago my husband announced, "Robins are building a nest in our firethorn bush. Watch and you will find some writing material."

"What lesson do they teach?" I asked.

"Diligence," he answered.

I agreed as I watched the robins fly across the yard to find straw for their new home.

I like to watch geese fly in "V" formation, each one flapping his wings to create an upward lift to the goose that follows. They teach a lesson on working together.

One day, after a snowstorm, I watched a bird scout out our bird feeder, then cautiously swoop down to claim a sunflower seed. Later, he returned with three other birds. *He's a good witness,* I thought, *bringing others to enjoy what he has found.* That's a good lesson on inviting people to church where they can find food for their souls.

Jesus said, "Are not two sparrows sold for a penny? Yet not one of them will fall to the ground apart from the will of your Father" (Matt. 10:29). What does that say to you?

O God, I am awed at Your classroom and the things You are teaching me.

Dividing

For the word of God is living and active.
Sharper than any double-edged sword,
it penetrates even to
dividing soul and spirit,
joints and marrow;
it judges the thoughts
and attitudes of the heart.

Hebrews 4:12

WHO ARE YOU?

Each of us has a story to tell. Each one is different. Some sound like ancient history while others read like a modern day novel. We are still writing our stories. Over, ever so many years, we sketch and fill in the details of our lives, embellishing them as we go along. The important thing is that each story end well.

Have you ever made a personal coat-of-arms? I have one stashed away that I use, on occasion, to introduce myself when I speak to women's groups. In the center of my coat-of-arms is a picture of me. I am a combination of whatever God gave me in the beginning, such as the color of my eyes and the length of my nose, shaped by the environment in which I grew up, and changed from time to time by the people and circumstances that have come into my life.

Clara Booth Luce said, "Every man's life can be reduced to one sentence." How do you want your epitaph to read?

Alfred Bernhard Nobel was surprised to read his own obituary in the newspaper one morning. Actually, it was his older brother who had died. The erroneous account of his death had a lasting effect on Nobel. Wanting to be remembered as a man of peace, he initiated the Nobel Prize, saying, "Every man ought to have the chance to correct his epitaph in midstream and write a new one."[xi]

The important question is not so much Who am I? but Whose am I? As Christians, we are "fellow citizens with God's people and members of God's household" (Eph. 2:19).

That's quite a heritage! Let's claim our citizenship in God's family and enjoy the benefits that are ours.

Thank You, O God, for adopting me into your royal family.

THE BIG PICTURE

Every fall my sister and brother and their spouses come for a visit. One tradition we three ladies have is to put together a puzzle. We sit around the table in our sunroom and talk while we look for special shapes and colors. Always, we have the box top displayed so we can see how the finished picture will look.

You've heard the story of the six blind men who were brought to see an elephant. Each man gave his assessment based on the part of the animal that he touched. The side became a wall; the tusk, a spear; the trunk, a snake; the leg, a tree; the ear, a fan; and the tail, a rope. Too bad they couldn't see the whole picture, but that's not always possible.

Joseph was thrown into a pit by his brothers and sold into slavery to an Egyptian caravan. The puzzle wasn't fitting together. But years later, Joseph was able to say to his brothers, who came to Egypt looking for grain, "God sent me ahead of you to preserve for you a remnant on earth and to save your lives by a great deliverance" (Gen. 45:7). It's a long story, but the pieces finally came together.

Have you found some missing pieces scattered throughout your life? When I was sixteen, I was in a serious automobile accident. It was not a fun year for me. Four years later when the insurance money enabled me to enroll in a Christian college, I understood better Romans 8:28 – "And we know that in all things God works for the good of those who love him, who have been called according to his purpose."

Over a period of seventy or eighty years, maybe less, we plan, sketch, and fill in the details of our lives. Golden moments and rainbow days mingle with brown deserts and dark valleys. From these mixed colors, God can design a masterpiece.

Dear Lord, help me as I put the finishing touches on my life portrait.

WHAT WOULD JESUS DO?

Several years ago the letters WWJD began appearing around the country on bracelets, tee shirts, and other paraphernalia. My grandchildren bought into the fad. I trust the program originated from someone's sincere desire to ask *What Would Jesus Do*? rather than a desire for commercial gain.

It's not always easy to decide what Jesus would do in a given situation. As I thought about the matter, I perused the Gospels to take another look at Jesus, the Son of God. He forgave sins, healed the sick, fed the hungry, and raised the dead. He spoke up for widows and orphans, made friends with sinners, and taught with authority.

Much of what Jesus did stemmed from His divinity, so a better question for you and me to ask is "What would Jesus have *me* to do?" That makes it more personal and makes us accountable to God. It puts Jesus first and us last.

In our younger days of pastoring, a group of teens came to my husband and asked him whether a particular form of entertainment was right or wrong. My husband questioned, "Have you prayed about it?"

"No," answered one of the teens. "We know what Jesus would say."

Whatever our age, shallow spirituality has a way of showing through our flimsy excuses and human desires. It pushes us to the sidelines and keeps us on the defensive.

"Do not conform any longer to the pattern of this world," the Bible tells us, "but be transformed by the renewing of your mind. Then you will be able to test and approve what God's will is – his good, pleasing and perfect will" (Rom. 12:2).

"*Mold me and make me after Thy will, While I am waiting, yielded and still*" (*Have Thine Own Way, Lord* by Adelaide A. Pollard).

BALANCING PRIORITIES

Priorities don't go away. They keep raising their heads and saying, "I'm first." If we aren't careful, we will listen to the loudest voices and not the more important ones that lay at our doorstep. It's easy to substitute convenient ways for obedient ways.

A handout from IDEA, a health and fitness source, says, "Living a balanced life is like surfing. You ride the waves of circumstances and try to stay balanced, but sometimes you get knocked off your board and go under."

It might help to write down our daily, weekly, and long-term goals, beginning with the most important. As Christians, loving God and serving Him tops our list. Under that, other roles come into play – spouse, parent, neighbor, employee, volunteer. There will be some "no matter what" items, such as keeping the Sabbath holy, caring for our families, loving our neighbors, being good citizens, creating "sacred time" for ourselves.

Keeping life synchronized is not always easy. Our local newspaper carried an article recently entitled, *Beliefs? Take Your Pick.* The article went on to say that most people who say they are Christians shape their own ideology. That's scary.

A sheep rancher, who lived alone on his Idaho ranch, found that his violin was out of tune a lot because he had no standard note to go by. He wrote to a radio station in California and asked if they would strike a particular note at a certain time each day. The radio station agreed, and the farmer was able to keep his violin tuned. Life is better when we live in harmony with the will of God.

Jesus said to His followers, "I am the way and the truth and the life. No one comes to the Father except through me" (John 14:6). Add this to your daily log.

O God, help me to keep "the main thing" the main thing.

I TALK TO MYSELF

Do you ever talk out loud to yourself? I do. Maybe that's more a woman's thing than a man's. I even answer myself sometimes.

As I look into the freezer – "What are we going to have for supper? Let's see, there's chicken, fish, and hamburger meat." Then I choose. The conversation becomes part of the decision making process.

"Where did I leave my purse? I'll check the car first."

"Remember to turn off the stove. Okay, I'd better set the timer."

I've never read a scientific treatise on why people talk to themselves, but I think it's quite simple. When we get older, we don't talk with other people as much, so it's just nice to hear a human voice. Then, too, an oral statement can reinforce a passing thought.

"Pleasant words are a honeycomb, sweet to the soul and healing to the bones" (Proverbs 16:24). The key word is *pleasant*. Whether we are talking on the phone, to the child next door, or to ourselves, we should speak kindly and wisely.

I like to pray out loud. Do you? I don't do it at night when my husband is asleep, but I do like to raise my voice in praise and petition when my only audience is God.

I enjoy singing to myself too – "I am loved, you are loved" (Bill Gaither).

To God, I sing, "I am Thine, O Lord; I have heard Thy voice, And it told Thy love to me" (Fanny Crosby).

"My mouth is filled with your praise," sang the Psalmist (Psalm 71:8a). Without an audience, let's quote some scripture, sing a praise chorus, or shout "Alleluia." God is listening.

O Lord, whether alone or in a group, may my words glorify You.

MAKING MEMORIES

From childhood to youth to old age we all build memories. Our memories are our very own – the places we've lived, the things we've done, the people we know. Many of them center on home and childhood. Was it the twenties, the forties, the eighties?

Certain moments and events in life pull out these feelings and emotions tucked away in obscure places. For me, these tingling sensations erupt at the first snowfall. They romp through my mind as I watch dying embers in the fireplace or walk through leaves on an autumn day. They emerge at Christmas and weddings and family reunions. They jump out when I look at photo albums, scrapbooks, and homemade videos.

Not all memories are good. Some hang like a rope around our neck. Forget the forgiven past, the failures, the "what ifs." Pull out the memories that make you smile and want to praise the Lord. As Paul reminds us, "– if anything is excellent or praiseworthy – think about such things" (Phil. 4:8b).

Since memory is a tool given by God, perhaps we should sharpen it by learning to use it more effectively. Even good memories can sometimes bind us in such a way that we find it difficult to enjoy the present. We may have to strategize to get back on track. Try something new and challenging. Vacation in a different place. Go back to school. Make life so interesting that you will have something fresh to share when you get together with family and friends.

Develop closeness to God through daily meditation, prayer, and Bible reading. Memorize some promises that mean a lot to you. Quote them at midnight when the world looks dark. Let your memory work for you, not against you.

Dear Father, help me to build good memories. They may be around a long time.

WHO IS MY NEIGHBOR?

The great storyteller, Dr. J.B. Chapman, told about a man who had such disagreeable neighbors that he decided to move west. When he came to a community that looked promising, he stopped at a country store and asked, "What kind of folks live around here?" The storekeeper questioned, "What kind of neighbors did you have where you came from?" The man stated that they were awful. The storekeeper replied, "That's the same kind of people you'll find here."

Another man who came by with the same question told the storekeeper, "We had the best neighbors you could find anywhere." The storekeeper responded, "That's exactly the kind we have in our area." This illustration reminds us that life has a boomerang effect.

Jesus told His followers "love your neighbor as yourself" (Matt. 19:18b). When a Jewish lawyer asked, "Who is my neighbor?" Jesus gave the parable of the Good Samaritan (Luke 10). Children like to act out this story of the man on the road to Jericho, who was robbed and beaten (They enact this part with gusto). Then the priest and Levite shake their heads as they walk by. The Good Samaritan comes along, binds up the man's wounds (band aids work here), put him on his donkey (use your imagination) and take him to an inn.

So, who is my neighbor? It may be the family across the street, a friend, or a stranger – anyone who needs help. We all know people who have been robbed and beaten by the circumstances of life. Do they need a babysitter, transportation to chemo treatments, a food pounding, someone to listen and pray with them? Being a good neighbor takes time and energy. Jesus showed us how to do it.

O God, help me to be a good neighbor to those who need me.

GUARD THE FLAME

The word *fireplace* can be traced to the Latin word for *focus*. In earlier days, the fireplace truly was the focal point of the home. Some of our family's happiest times have taken place around the fireplace on winter evenings as we watched flames flicker patterns on the ceiling.

In one parsonage we did not have a fireplace; so, for Christmas one year we purchased an artificial one. It looked quite authentic and even simulated the crackling of a fire. But it wasn't the same.

In the Bible, fire is sometimes used as a symbol of God's presence. Moses stopped at a burning bush to receive a divine assignment. Isaiah, touched by a coal from God's altar, changed from spectator to fiery prophet. The one hundred and twenty in the Upper Room were transformed from cowards to bold witnesses as flames danced on their heads.

A woman, who went to visit a silver smith, watched as he held a piece of silver over the hottest part of the fire. "I do that to refine the silver and burn away the impurities," the silver smith commented.

"How do you know when the silver is refined?" the lady asked.

The man replied, "Oh, that's easy – when I see my image in it."

Referring to the coming Messiah, the prophet Malachi wrote, "He will sit as a refiner and a purifier of silver . . . That they may offer to the Lord an offering of righteousness" (Mal. 3:3, NKJV).

The fire of the Holy Spirit cannot be faked, like our Montgomery Ward's fireplace. Let's guard the flame carefully.

Dear Jesus, thank You for bringing light into our dark world.

THE TIME FACTOR

What is time? Is it just another day on the calendar? Is it an endless routine or a daily appointment with self-centered goals? Is time a robber of life, drawing us closer to our destiny? Or, could time be a blank check, a road less traveled, a prelude to something great? Could God be at work this very day to make time your friend?

Most of my life I have lived by the clock. That's neither good nor bad. I have things to do, calls to make, letters to write. I have books to read, lessons to study, bills to pay.

Benjamin Franklin wrote, "Dost thou love life? Then do not squander time, for that is the stuff life is made of."

Job wrote, "My days are swifter than a weaver's shuttle, and they come to an end without hope" (Job 7:6). I have experienced the swiftness Job felt, but not the hopelessness. In the end, Job himself came to a better understanding of life.

At my age, time seems to be slowing down a bit. There are fewer people around and not as much traveling. There's less baking and scrubbing. The phone doesn't ring as often; the mailbox contains mostly flyers. Of course, things still get hectic around Christmas, leaf-raking time, and doctor's visits. Overall, I'm thankful for the change.

Time is important. Hours, days, and weeks make up life. How many years do you and I have left on planet earth? Only God knows. We do have something to say about the quality of our lives as we make right choices and depend on the Holy Spirit to lead us. Life is a gift – all of it. So enjoy.

Thank You, O God, for this moment in time. Help me to accomplish the things I need to do today. Show me how to use any leftover time wisely. Thank You that I can spend more time with You.

HOW MUCH MONEY DO WE NEED?

Money and other forms of bargaining power govern much of our world today. How much or how little we need depends on a lot of factors, some beyond our control. Many people around the world eke out an existence while others amass a fortune. Most of us are somewhere in between.

I grew up on a farm where my parents raised our food, made our clothes, and used homemade remedies for most illnesses. They ground corn into meal, washed on a scrub board, and walked for transportation. To pay the doctor or cancel a debt, they would sometimes sell a pig. It's still like that in some parts of the world today.

A person's style of retirement living depends, in part, on money accumulated, inherited, or even borrowed. For many of us that includes Social Security benefits. Every day I thank God for a comfortable home, a dependable car, and enough food and clothes.

We pay our tithe and enjoy giving to the children and grandchildren. The only reason I would want more is so I could give more.

Many senior adults do have legitimate questions concerning finances. Will our retirement fund run out? Will we have to downsize again? Will my spouse or I need extended health care? While I was dwelling on these questions recently, God seemed to say, "Just trust me and live one day at a time."

"I can do that," I replied.

Jesus says to all of us, "But seek first his kingdom and his righteousness, and all these things will be given to you" (Matt. 6:33). I claim that promise today.

Thank You, Lord, for the 75 years You have supplied my needs, filled in the gaps, and produced unexpected resources. I place tomorrow in your hands.

WHAT IS BEAUTY?

An old adage says that beauty is in the eyes of the beholder. I hope that's true because the older we get the more outside beauty loses its shape, color, and texture. Eyelids, cheeks, and other anatomy drop. Smooth skin gives way to wrinkles. Shiny hair turns gray. Stooped shoulders and arthritic joints alter gait. Hugh Downs wrote, "Youth is a gift of nature. Old age is a work of art."

We all admire the softness of a baby's skin, the bright eyes of a child, the agile movements of the young; but those of us who are fortunate do grow old. I sometimes answer my grandchildren's questions by simply saying, "My body is wearing out." I think that may be a little scary to them.

One Christmas, several years ago, my husband asked for a large portrait to be made of me from a photograph taken during my college days. I knew what he was thinking, but I went along anyway. So, today a picture of a smiling coed hangs on our dining room wall along side my husband's youthful counterpart.

Though we always want to look our best, Peter reminds us that beauty "should not come from outward adorning . . . Instead, it should be that of your inner self, the unfading beauty of a gentle and quiet spirit, which is of great worth in God's sight" (1 Peter 3:3-4). I like Peter's description of beauty for all ages. I might even qualify.

Dr. Leslie Parrot wrote, "The personality change many people need is not a face lift but a heart lift."[xii] That would sure get people's attention.

I saw a cartoon recently that echoes that thought: "A smile is a face lift that's in anyone's price range." Look in the mirror, smile, and see what happens.

Dear Father, let the beauty of Jesus be seen in me.

IN HIS STEPS

Charles Sheldon in his book, *IN HIS STEPS*, tells a graphic story about Henry Maxwell, the pastor of a prestigious church, and some of his members who took a one year vow to ask before doing anything, "What would Jesus do?" Among those making the pledge were Pastor Maxwell, the editor of the daily newspaper, the railroad superintendent, the president of a local college, a merchant, a doctor, an author, an heiress, and a gifted singer. How these and others wrestled with the question, "What would Jesus do?" creates a transforming narrative of compassion and change. Oh, that this would be the story of today's church.

Eliza Hewitt wrote, "Trying to walk in the steps of the Savior, Trying to follow my Savior and King, Shaping our lives by His blessed example, Happy, how happy the songs that we bring!" As Christians, we are not trying to be clones of each other, but we do want to be Christlike in what we do and say.

A father was plodding through the snow to get to the barn when he heard a little voice behind him call, "Wait, Daddy. I'm following you." He looked back to see his son trying to place his small shoes in Dad's big tracks. The father was stricken with remorse because he knew that he was not a good example for his son. He asked God for forgiveness and became a better role model.

The Psalmist wrote, "When I said 'my foot is slipping,' your love, O God, supported me" (Psalm 94:18). Do you sometimes feel like you are slipping? If so, take courage. God's love calls out again and again – through the Bible and the great cloud of witnesses in Hebrews 12:1 – "Keep on coming, You're almost here. You're doing great!"

Dear Lord, help me to follow you closely so that I will not lead anyone else astray.

WHAT IS SUCCESS?

"What is your definition of success?" I asked my husband this week as we were flying 38,000 feet in the air on our way home from attending the 50th anniversary of a church we had pastored.

"Personal success, for me," he replied, "is reaching the place where I am fulfilled mentally, socially, and spiritually." That's a tall order. Coming from my husband, I knew his answer included lots of hard work, goal setting, and accomplishment.

Some anonymous poet has written:

Isn't it strange that princes and kings,
And clowns that caper in sawdust rings,
And common folks like you and me,
Are builders of eternity?
Each is given a bag of tools,
A shapeless mass, and a book of rules,
And each must build ere life has flown,
A stumbling block or a stepping stone!

According to the above poem, success is paved with steppingstones that say to those following us, "This is the way; walk in it" (Isaiah 30:21b). Success, then, is not so much about achievement; it's a godly lifestyle that helps to shape our families, our jobs, our communities, our churches, even our world.

We cannot judge our own degree of success. One generation will commend its works to another. The important thing is that God gives His "thumps-up."

O God, help me to make a difference in my world.

DIVISION OF LABOR

You've heard the little ditty about four people named Everybody, Somebody, Nobody, and Anybody. When there was a job to be done, Everybody thought Somebody would do it. Actually, Anybody could have done it, but Nobody did.

Homes, churches, businesses, and governments need a division of labor. It's important for people to know what their job is so they can learn to do it well. There's always some overlapping as we help co-workers and broaden our skills, but assigned responsibilities come first.

In the home, the division of labor often becomes blurred. Most women today have careers outside the home, which means family members share household duties. In retirement, individual roles merge even more. I still like to cook and keep an orderly household while my husband maintains the lawn, takes care of the car, and runs errands. Nevertheless, it's great when he vacuums, and I can help manicure the flowerbeds.

A little girl wrote a letter to God and asked Him if His angels did all His work. "Mommy calls us her angels," she said, "but we have to do everything."

None of us have elves show up to wash the dishes or mow the lawn, but I do hope you have someone – a son or daughter or a person from your church or neighborhood – to help do the things you cannot do for yourself. That happens to my husband and me often.

God's Word says, "And whatever you do, whether in word or deed, do it all in the name of the Lord Jesus, giving thanks to God the Father through him" (Col. 3:17).

So whether you are caring for a sick spouse, crocheting an afghan for a granddaughter, or leading a Bible study, you are doing it as unto the Lord.

Dear Father, help me to carry out the assignment you have given to me.

WHAT IS RIGHT, LORD?

I remember, as a child, seeing a picture of a man walking along a highway, who stopped at a crossroads to get his bearing. One sign said, "My Way"; the other said, "God's Way." Most of you reading this article chose God's way a long time ago; however, there are countless other choices and decisions to make as we continue our journey through life.

In today's comic strip, Garfield was lying on his back in the sun taking it easy. He said to himself, "It feels good lying here, but I'm hungry, and there's a good show on TV . . . What to do?" Many of our decisions are small, like Garfield's, and I think God says, "Do what you want to." But there are some options that shape our destiny and breed *good* or *evil* in those around us. Concerning these, James writes, "If any of you lacks wisdom, he should ask God, who gives generously to all without finding fault, and it will be given to him" (James 1:5).

Helen Temple, in one of her insightful poems, wrote, "How can I know what's really right? There don't seem to be any sharp lines between right and wrong anymore." Have you ever felt that way?

In *The Christian's Secret of a Happy Life*, Hannah Whitall Smith wrote, "There are four ways in which He (God) reveals His will to us – through Scriptures, through providential circumstances, through the convictions of our own higher judgment, and through the inward impressions of the Holy Spirit on our minds. Where these four harmonize, it is safe to say that God speaks."[xiii] That's good advice for all ages.

Guide me, O Thou great Jehovah, Pilgrim thro' this barren land. I am weak, but Thou art mighty; Hold me with Thy pow'rful hand (William Williams).

MAIL CALL

Professional writers fill our mailboxes with requests for money, credit card offers, and magazine subscriptions. However, personal letter writing is becoming a lost art. When was the last time you received a letter from family or friends? Was it Christmas time?

I do appreciate our modern system of instant communication. Last week I e-mailed our grandson, who is an exchange student in England. I call my sister, in a distant state, often to check on a health problem. I dialed 911 not long ago and received a quick response. Nevertheless, I still enjoy receiving letters. I can hold a letter in my hand, recognize the writing, read it again and again.

We have a large container of special letters that we have received through the years. As I thought about this article, I reread a few of them. The first one was from my Father, written 44 years ago several weeks before he died. He closed the letter with the words, "Frances, I love the Lord so much. Tell the children hello. God be with you till we meet in heaven. Love, Daddy." My Dad did not accept the Lord until ten months before he died. No wonder I cherish that letter!

In a way, the Bible is God's letter to us, containing 66 books written over a period of 1,600 years by more than 40 authors, whom God used to get His message to the world. Why not read one of Paul's letters today? Or Peter's? Read John's statement in his letter to believers, "How great is the love the Father has lavished on us, that we should be called children of God!" (1 John 3:1a). I'm glad John wrote that.

Uh-uh, it's 2:00, mail time. I'll take a walk to our mailbox and look for – yes, a letter – and smile. I hope you get one too.

Dear Father, thank You for your Love Letter to me. I read it often.

AUDIO-VISUAL CHRISTIANS

Do you recall the first radio you bought or your first record player? Remember your black and white television? Media technology has come a long way in our lifetime. I, for one, can't keep up with it. Just when I mastered e-mailing, my grandchildren graduated to cell phones with text messaging. I'm not there yet.

I do enjoy audio-visuals. As a Sunday School teacher, I used filmstrips (outdated, I know), pictures, recordings, slides, charts, and role playing to make the lesson come alive. Today, we live in a world of Power Point presentations, video clips, and drama productions. Sometimes, we older adults have a hard time processing it all.

After repeated warnings and repairs on my old computer (my first), I bought a new one on sale last week. A friend spent several hours installing it and, in the process, downloaded *Goggle Earth.* He demonstrated it by showing me aerial views of the Grand Canyon and Paris, France, then zooming in on my own neighborhood. Wow! We talked about how amazing, yet how scary such technology can be.

We live in Charlotte, North Carolina, home of the Billy Graham Library. Three times we have taken out-of-town visitors to enjoy the multi-media presentation of Dr. Graham's life and ministry. It's a powerful, moving experience. You need to see it.

Jesus told His disciples, "In the same way, let your light shine before men, that they may see your good deeds and praise your Father in heaven" (Matt. 5:16).

Are we audio-visual Christians? Can those around us see Jesus in us? Are we lighting the way for them? Or, do we need to clean our lenses and zoom in closer? God, the Holy Spirit, will help us do that.

Dear God, help me to be an audio-visual Christian as I live and talk "Jesus."

WHAT ARE YOU AFRAID OF?

Each age group has its own set of fears. Children are afraid of loud noises, separation from parents, monsters hiding in the closet or under the bed. Adolescents may be afraid of rejection, poor grades, or the neighborhood bully. Adults address job changes, divorce, break-ins, and stolen identities. According to counselors, certain fears are normal and may even be necessary for psychological development.

As senior adults, we have our own concerns. (*Concern* sounds more religious than *fear*). Our list might include cancer, the death of a spouse, living alone, dwindling finances. We are concerned about the needs of our children and grandchildren.

The Bible tells us, "There is no fear in love. But perfect love drives out fear, because fear has to do with punishment. The one who fears is not made perfect in love" (1 John 4:18). Theologians tell us this Scripture refers to the Final Judgment. The person who is motivated by love for God can stand before Him unafraid. I don't think many Christians fear death itself. It's the "getting there" that gnaws us. We don't want to be a burden, a dead-end case for our families. Neither do we welcome pain.

David wrote, "When I am afraid, I will trust in you" (Psalm 56:3). That's the key: knowing God well enough to trust Him in our times of illness, bereavement, and change. A sign on an inn in England stated, "Fear knocked at the door; faith answered. No one was there."

A senior version of *Jesus Loves Me* says, "Jesus loves me, this I know though my hair is white as snow. Though my sight is growing dim still He bids me trust in Him."

Write down your greatest fear, and then sing this song with me. Don't you feel better?

Dear Father, thank You for your guardian angels.

MAKE THE WORLD GO AWAY

I remember, as a teenager, sitting in our front porch swing on warm summer evenings and listening to Eddie Arnold sing *Make the World Go Away*. Have you ever shared those sentiments? What would you like to push over the brink of the universe?

My personal list includes home invasions in my part of town, identity theft, and the hidden agendas of some politicians. I'd like to erase war, disease, prejudice, and terrorism. Let's go the extra mile and eliminate birth defects, mental confusion, and poverty.

A weary father came home one evening and sat down with the newspaper to rest a few minutes, when into his lap jumped his five-year-old son. Though he loved his son dearly, he needed some time to unwind. With a flash of insight, he picked up a page of the newspaper containing a huge picture of earth and asked his son to bring a pair of scissors and some tape. The father cut the picture into a jigsaw puzzle and told his son, "Put the world back together and then we will play. OK?"

Quickly the lad taped everything into place and ran back to his father, who asked, "How did you do it so quickly?"

"It was easy, Dad," he replied. "There was a picture of a man on the back, and when I put the man together, the world came together." Christ is the answer to the brokenness in our world today.

I read it again this morning – "Then I saw a new heaven and a new earth, for the first heaven and the first earth had passed away" (Rev. 21:1a). Can you imagine a world without sin, an eternal Garden of Eden? Heaven will be that and so much more. Are you ready?

O God, thank You for the Holy Spirit that helps us to live right in our kind of world.

GETHSEMANE

I still remember the thought-provoking outline, given by Dr. Leslie Parrot, for a Bible lesson based on Jesus' experience in the Garden of Gethsemane on the night before His crucifixion.

1. Everyone will have his/her own Gethsemane.
2. It will probably occur in a familiar place.
3. There may be a Judas in the picture.
4. You'll probably feel all alone in your Gethsemane.
5. God will meet you there.

I hope your mind isn't reeling as you think of unpleasant events, hurtful statements, and faces of people you had rather forget. Most of us have encountered some ridicule and may have been the subject of someone's gossip. But we've not been martyred for our faith or left to suffer alone.

You've probably read the story of Leonardo da Vinci's struggle as he painted his famous *Last Supper*. Before he began the work, he quarreled violently with a fellow painter and ended up painting the man's face as that of Judas. He then found that he could not paint the face of Christ. After forgiving his antagonist and changing the face of Judas, he was able to successfully finish his masterpiece.

In Gethsemane Jesus prayed, "My Father, if it is possible, may this cup be taken from me. Yet not as I will, but as you will" (Matt. 26:39b). Can you pray that? Will you forgive your Judas? Gethsemane is a place of decision, a place of surrender, a place where Christ can meet us and give victory over sin and death.

All to Thee, my blessed Savior, I surrender all (Joseph W. Van DeVenter).

HOW IS YOUR STRESS LEVEL?

Are you one of those laid back persons who nap during commercial breaks and fall asleep the moment your head hits the pillow? Or, are you more hyper and sometimes strain at the bit as you face the tensions of the day? Psychologists tell us that stress is a normal part of life caused by both positive and negative events. Our responses to these stressors depend on our personality, genes, and past experiences. This means that even Christians may react differently to a given situation.

Since I have an active mind that doesn't automatically shut down at 9:00 in the evening, I have to work at relaxing. I know that's a paradox, but I am gaining ground. I have several brochures that remind me to keep a positive mental attitude, get enough rest, exercise, and eat right. As I get older, I find that I need to simplify life and take more breaks throughout the day – time to make a telephone call, read a chapter in a book, or walk around the yard. I've learned some stretching exercises and foot rubs. I even bought some lavender bubble bath the other day and drink chamomile tea occasionally. I'd rather slow down gradually than crash at the bottom of the hill.

Jesus said, "Come to me, all you who are weary and burdened, and I will give you rest. Take my yoke upon you and learn from me, for I am gentle and humble in heart, and you will find rest for your souls. For my yoke is easy and my burden is light" (Matt. 11:28-30).

Come – I like that. It's a good prescription for any age, an antidote for every season of life. It invites us into the Lord's presence where we can find rest for both soul and body.

Dear Lord, thank You for making me "lie down in green pastures" and leading me "beside quiet waters" (Psalm 23:2).

ROUT THE ENEMY

Peter wrote to Christians in the first century, "Be self-controlled and alert. Your enemy the devil prowls around like a roaring lion looking for someone to devour" (1 Peter 5:8).

That's true in the twenty first century too. Sometimes we get Satan confused with people, organizations, and political parties, but evil is still the enemy. Satan worms his way in, like he did in the Garden of Eden, to ask questions and cast doubt on the sovereignty of God. He comes at our weakest moments, offering non–biblical solutions and causing us to blame others for our problems.

Job, in the Old Testament, had a showdown with Satan as his world came tumbling down. Believe it or not, his friends came to help Satan out. That might happen in your case. But Job kept his faith and stood exonerated in the end.

Jesus had clashes with Satan, beginning with his wilderness temptation and climaxing in the Garden of Gethsemane. He showed us how to overcome the Tempter by praying, quoting Scripture, and depending on the Heavenly Father.

Have you ever struggled with Satan? I remember one long ago night when my husband wrestled with unseen forces as we sat in our living room reading the Scriptures and praying throughout the night. With dawn, came release and the assurance that God was in control.

I remember other times when I've said, "Get behind me, Satan," as he brought up suggestions I knew were not from God.

Paul wrote, "Put on the full armor of God so that you can take your stand against the devil's schemes" (Eph. 6:11). Let's buckle our armor tighter and keep fighting.

Holy Spirit, thank You for equipping me for the battles of life.

TAKE UP YOUR CROSS

Crosses come in different shapes and sizes. Some are worn around the neck on a chain. Others adorn churches – both wayside chapels and ancient cathedrals. In the first century, the Romans used crosses to execute criminals. God used a cross to save the world.

Near the close of Jesus' public ministry He turned to the crowd following Him and said, "If anyone would come after me, he must deny himself and take up his cross and follow me" (Matt. 16:24).

What kind of cross, Lord? The decorative kind or the suffering kind? Many in the crowd must have asked that question because, one by one, they began to walk away. We like gold crosses, padded crosses, smooth crosses – crosses that don't burden us down or make us stand out in a hostile crowd.

Jesus' early disciples soon learned that Jesus' cross was their cross. To identify with Christ was to lay their lives on the line and cling to the truth of the Gospel no matter what happened. Christ's mission to save the world became their mission. Paul wrote, "I have been crucified with Christ and I no longer live, but Christ lives in me" (Gal. 2:20a).

People still die for their faith. You and I will probably not be in that group. However, faith does not make us immune to trouble. What kind of cross might you be bearing today? Whatever it may be, we can develop the kind of faith Job had when he declared, "Though he slay me, yet will I hope in him" (Job 13:15a). At that point, the message of the cross breaks through.

"Must Jesus bear the cross alone, and all the world go free? No, there's a cross for ev-'ry-one, And there's a cross for me" (Thomas Shepherd and others).

Dear Jesus, thank You for walking the "Calvary Road" for me.

BANE OR BLESSING?

A bane is something bad; a blessing is something good. At the onset, it's sometimes hard to tell the difference. Good sometimes turns bad, and bad can become good. That's why we need lots of wisdom, discernment, and patience as we face life in today's world.

The boll weevil, a bane to cotton farmers, crossed into Texas from Mexico about 1890. Farmers were forced to plant other crops and use some of their land for raising cattle, hogs, and chickens. As a result, many farmers became more prosperous than when they raised only cotton.

In Titusville, Pennsylvania, a farmer's cows wouldn't drink from the creek because it was covered with slime. A new owner bought the farm for $830 and discovered oil. Thus Quaker State was born. That which was a bane for one became a blessing to another.

On January 12, 1915, the Hall brothers' greeting card warehouse in Kansas City burned to the ground. The entire inventory was lost. The two young brothers considered quitting, then decided to borrow more money and buy a local engraving firm so they could design and print their own greeting cards. Today, Hallmark turns out millions of greeting cards each day.

Looking back, we can all recall times when God entered the picture and changed the status quo. It might have been a job change, a cross-country move, or an accident. In the process, we learn to trust when we cannot see and to thank God for the impossible.

King David knew what it was to be physically weak, emotionally drained, and spiritually exhausted. Time and again he cried for help and God rescued him. "The Lord is a refuge for the oppressed," he wrote, "a stronghold in times of trouble" (Psalm 9:9).

O God, thank You for helping me to make some "U" turns in my life.

SMALL THINGS MATTER

A famous explorer in South America was equipped to meet wild animals, snakes, and crocodiles; these were no threat. However, he failed to consider the millions of chiggers that eventually foiled the expedition.

A forest fire that destroyed over 18,000 acres was started when a woman burned a "Dear John" letter and wept while the fire spread.

Solomon wrote, "Catch for us the foxes, the little foxes that ruin the vineyards" (Song of Songs 2:15a). Sensual thoughts, unkind words, procrastination, lack of daily devotions, watching too much television, and a lot of other things can become foxes that spoil our testimonies and make us vulnerable to Satan's evil suggestions.

On the other hand, little things can enrich life, enhance a relationship, and show Jesus to those around us. A smile, a friendly word, a sympathetic nod, an invitation to church, or a batch of cookies can help open doors. Brick by brick, churches are built, homes are strengthened, and the Kingdom of God goes forth.

What gives you a lift – a spring morning bathed in pastels; fleecy white clouds skimming across a blue sky; leaves rustling in the still of the night; the mockingbird's song? Do you like to eat at your favorite restaurant, visit relatives, read a good book?

Do you enjoy meeting with your church family on Sunday mornings to sing praises to God for these treasures, and others that we often take for granted?

Abraham Lincoln wrote, "In the dew of little things the heart finds its meaning and is refreshed." I think I'll make a list of the things that refresh me this week and offer it as a gift to God. Maybe you would like to do that too.

Thank You, dear Father, for the little things that make life good.

LEAVE IT IN GOD'S HANDS

I remember the first canoe trip I took with my husband many years ago while on vacation in Arkansas. Was I scared? Yes, even though I could see bottom most of the way. We enjoyed stretches of smooth rowing along shaded passageways beneath age-old trees. Occasionally, stumps and low-hanging branches slowed our progress. Several times we got stuck on rocks and had to get out and push. We even went in circles, sideways, and backwards a time or two. Aren't you glad you weren't along?

About halfway through our canoe trip my husband convinced me to take my oar out of the water and let him guide the craft by himself. Amazingly, things went better. The tension was gone, and we again headed in the right direction.

I've discovered that life is like that. Some days are perfect; others are filled with frustrations, struggles, even an occasional upheaval. Have you been there? I remember one rocky stretch when I cried, "Help!" and God gave me a promise from Isaiah 43:19: "See, I am doing a new thing! Now it springs up; do you not perceive it? I am making a way in the desert and streams in the wasteland." For many years I have displayed this promise on a refrigerator magnet to remind me that God is always working. I just read it again and said "Thank You."

A.B. Simpson wrote, "Much of the life of faith consists in letting things alone." Sometimes there's nothing else we can say or do to solve a problem or mend a relationship. It's then that we put the matter in God's hands and walk away. That's not a cop out, but an act of faith in the One whose hands created the universe, stopped the mouths of lions, and raised the dead. He's looking out for us too. Trust Him.

O God, hold me steady when the going gets rough.

GROW OLD ALONG WITH ME

Robert Browning wrote, "Grow old along with me. The best is yet to be – the last of life for which the first was made."

What is the magic age? Is it 25? 50? 65? In colonial America life expectancy was 35 years. Those 65 and older represented only two percent of the population; therefore, elderly people were highly revered and sought out as advisors. Can you believe that, in those days, both men and women tried to look older?

We've outlived that generation and, today, youth is prized. Senior adults, however, still have an important role in the home and society. Our grandchildren love us, our church needs us, and the nation's economy depends on us.

Pickles had a cute cartoon recently. Grandpa interrupted his grandson, Nelson, to give a lecture on how young people should respect their elders who are much older and wiser. When he finished, he asked his grandson what he wanted to tell him. "I just wanted to say you've got your shirt on inside out," Nelson replied.

Sometimes the truth humbles us; nevertheless, lots of myths surround old age, too. Old age does not always begin at 65; most older adults are not in poor health; only 10 percent of people over 65 show significant memory loss; and older workers can still learn to do a job well. The best cosmetic in the world is an active mind that is always learning something new.

Old age does not equate spiritual maturity, but the two should go together. Peter wrote, "But grow in the grace and knowledge of our Lord and Savior Jesus Christ" (2 Peter 3:18a). I want to do that, Lord.

O God, help me to grow old gracefully.

DEATH HAS LOST ITS STING

I stood in the hospital intensive care unit by the bedside of my friend, Betty, along with her husband and two of her adult children. The time had come. All we could do was watch, pray, and sing. We did all three.

The day before Betty's cerebral hemorrhage, she and I had talked for hours. In one of her serious moments, Betty stated, "In God's economy, nothing is ever lost; God takes every pain, every sorrow, even death itself and makes something new." I was glad I could share that with the huge crowd who came to celebrate Betty's life a few days later.

The Apostle Paul wrote, "Death has been swallowed up in victory. Where, O death, is your victory? Where, O death, is your sting?" (1 Cor. 15:54b-55).

In his last book, Bill Bright, founder and president of Campus Crusade for Christ, chronicled his journey from terminal illness to victory over death. In the first chapter he wrote, "I am on the last mile, but I am not alone. The Lord Jesus by His Holy Spirit is with me, and the knowledge of his presence dispels the darkness and allays any fears."[xiv]

A friend, in one of our pastorates, told me how she had been declared clinically dead and was then resuscitated. She talked of the light and the all-consuming love and peace that enveloped her. "One thing for sure," she said, "I'll never fear death again."

One of the prayers we teach our children is *Now I Lay Me Down to Sleep.* To be honest, not many children die in their sleep. I think this prayer is for older people like you and me. Let's pray it together.

Now I lay me down to sleep. I pray Thee, Lord, my soul to keep. If I should die before I wake, I pray Thee, Lord, my soul to take. Amen and amen.

See you yonder.

Frances Simpson

About the Author

Frances Simpson was born on a cotton farm in Alabama during the depression years. As a minister's wife, she has seen the world from different angles – the beaches of Florida, the farmlands of Indiana, the wheat fields of Kansas, the snows of Ohio, and the mountains of North Carolina. She and her husband now live in Charlotte, North Carolina, where they stay busy with home, church, and family activities.

This is Frances' third book. She has written numerous devotional articles and enjoys creating curriculum material for small group Bible studies. Frances writes, "I've lived long enough to watch God work. There's so much to see, to do, to feel, and to tell. That's why I like to write."

Frances' priorities these days are her husband, children, and grandchildren, who make life fun and give her a platform from which to write.

Notes

[i] R.A. Torrey, *The Power of Prayer* (Grand Rapids: Zondervan Publishing House, 1971), 17.

[ii] Glaphre Gilliland, *When the Pieces Don't Fit* (Grand Rapids: Zondervan Publishing House, 1984), 42.

[iii] Paul Lee Tan, *Encyclopedia of 7700 Illustrations* (Rockville: Assurance Publishers, 1979), 529.

[iv] *The Treasure Chest*, edited by Charles L. Wallis (New York: Harper & Row, 1965), 158.

[v] Wayne Dyer, "Being a Child Again," *Reader's Digest*, March 1981, 58.

[vi] Charles Hastings Smith, "THE LAST GOODBYE," *Herald of Holiness*, January 15, 1979, 6.

[vii] Fletcher Spruce, "The Four Faces of Easter," *STANDARD*, 1970.

[viii] Dan Boone, *UNSEEN POWERS*, edited by Everett Leadingham (Kansas City: Beacon Hill Press, 1999), 9.

[ix] Morris Chalfant, "I Hope You Live All Your Life," *STANDARD*, July 11, 2004.

[x] Newman Flower, "A Creed in a Garden," *In the Garden* (Nashville: NELSON REGENCY, 1994).

[xi] Doug Murren and Barb Shurin, *Is It Real When It Doesn't Work?*

[xii] Leslie Parrott, *The Habit of Happiness* (Waco, Texas: Word Books, 1987), 141.

[xiii] Hannah W. Smith, *The Christian's Secret of a Happy Life* (New York: Fleming H. Revell Co., 1883), 101.

[xiv] Bill Bright, *The Journey Home* (Nashville: Thomas Nelson Publishers, 2003), 4.